GOD

is

ALWAYS
AT WORK

Even When You Do Not Know It

Dr. Dino J. Pedrone

The book of Esther is magnificent. Esther, the Jewish queen, is a magnificent woman! She is a leader among leaders.

Her Persian name is Esther which means star. Her Jewish name is Hadassah meaning myrtle. The myrtle trees blossom is in the shape of a star. As a human being, Esther is truly a star of stars!

Mordecai is a man of honor. His loyalty to his people the Jews is to be cherished! He is a godly leader and influencer.

His prized pupil is Esther. His influence on her life saves a nation.

With all due respect to them the book of Esther is really about someone else. He is unnamed. This volume opens up a unique approach to the hero that provides deliverance to an entire people. "God is always at work....even when you do not know it!" Read and see if you agree!

DEDICATION

E sther is the story of a queen. She was a magnificent woman. I have a queen in my life. She is my wife. My wife does not remind me of Esther. Queen Esther reminds me of my wife.

Roberta Dee (Bobbi) Pedrone is an amazing woman. She and I have journeyed together. We dated, married, had children, grand-children, involved ourselves in 40 years of pastoral ministry and nearly 50 years of ministry. I cannot imagine going on this journey with anyone else but her. She is my queen and I affection-ately dedicate this volume to her. Thanks, Sweetheart for being the ultimate partner in my life.

TABLE OF CONTENTS

ESTHER

Who is Agag?

His name was Agag. He is first mentioned by Balaam in Numbers 24:7. While in the wilderness, as Balaam viewed the nation of Israel encamped according to their tribes, the Spirit of God came upon him and he took up his oracle and began to praise God. Agag was the powerful king of the Amalekites, a member of the ancient nomadic people of Canaan.

This nomadic people are first mentioned in Scripture in Genesis 14:7. The patriarch Abraham is chosen of God to inherit Canaan. In the Dead Sea area they were attacked. This people became a group of fighters. God taught the people of God disciplinary lessons. The Amalekites and the Canaanites who dwelt in the mountains, would regularly attack and drive the people back (Numbers 14:25). The Amalekites were often connected with the Canaanites.

It was the Amalekites who fought with Israel in Rephidim. This was the familiar and somewhat spectacular event of Moses holding his arms up while Israel fought. As long as his arms were up the Israelites prevailed over Amalek. When his hands became heavy Amalek prevailed. His colleagues, Aaron and Hur, supported Moses and held his hands up until sundown and the people of God prevailed.

When an altar was built it was both a place of worship and a reminder. An altar is built here and it is called "The Lord is my banner." It is interesting to note the Scripture (Exodus 17:14 -16)

"Then the Lord said to Moses, "Write this for a memorial in the book and recount it in the hearing of Joshua, that I will utterly blot out the remembrance of Amalek from under heaven." And Moses built an altar and called its name, The-Lord-Is-My-Banner; for he said, "Because the Lord has sworn: the Lord will have war with Amalek from generation to generation." These people would oppose God, His people, and His work. God said they were to be blotted out! The reminder is that from generation to generation there would be war between the Lord and Amalek.

Amalek was vicious. They had chosen to destroy Israel and even attacked those who were unable to fight. *"Remember what Amalek did to you on the way as you were coming out of Egypt, how he met you on the way and attacked your rear ranks, all the stragglers at your rear, when you were tired and weary; and he did not fear God. Therefore it shall be, when the Lord your God has given you rest from your enemies all around, in the land which the Lord your God is giving you to possess as an inheritance, that you will blot out the remembrance of Amalek from under heaven. You shall not forget."* (Deuteronomy 25:17-19) The people are again reminded to protect themselves and to destroy the enemy.

A lesson of the Old Testament that is often repeated is that God will allow evil nations to defeat Israel because of their disobedience. Such is the case recorded in Judges 3:12-13 *"And the children of Israel again did evil in the sight of the Lord. So the Lord strengthened Eglon king of Moab against Israel, because they had done evil in the sight of the Lord. Then he gathered to himself the people of Ammon and Amalek, went and defeated Israel, and took possession of the City of Palms."* The people of Amalek joined in to defeat Israel.

In the beautiful song of Deborah recorded in Judges 5 the nation of Amalek is mentioned as they lived in Ephraim. *"From Ephraim were those whose roots were in Amalek. After you, Benjamin, with your peoples, From Machir rulers came down, And from Zebulun those who bear the recruiter's staff."* (Judges 5:14) This was a nomadic group that would join with other nations to go against Israel.

This group was diametrically opposed to Israel and the teachings of Yahweh God. When there was a battle with them there was only one recourse. Israel must destroy the Amalekites. They are the enemy!

Eventually, Saul becomes the king of Israel. He established his sovereignty of the land. (I Samuel 15:47-52) He takes an army and attacks the Amalekites! Saul's war with them was with the added burden of fighting with the Philistines.

The prophet Samuel in obedience to God's command, anoints Saul to be the king. The Lord's word is very clear. *"Thus says the Lord of hosts: 'I will punish Amalek for what he did to Israel, how he ambushed him on the way when he came up from Egypt. Now go and attack Amalek, and utterly destroy all that they have, and do not spare them. But kill both man and woman, infant and nursing child, ox and sheep, camel and donkey."* (I Samuel 15:2-3)

Now, back to our man, Agag. He is now the king of the Amalekites. It is time for this battle. God's command is solid and sure! All must be destroyed! Saul obeys. He salvages a group who were friends with Amalek! The Kenites depart. The war is on. Down go the Amalekites! But wait a minute, Saul does the unthinkable, **"But Saul and the people spared Agag and the best** *of the sheep, the oxen, the fatlings, the lambs, and all that was good, and were unwilling to utterly destroy them. But everything despised and worthless, that they utterly destroyed."* (I Samuel 15:9) He spares the king and the best of the animals and the good things!

The result of his disobedience would last for years. God spoke to Samuel and the prophet confronted the king. Notice the conversation *" Now the word of the Lord came to Samuel, saying, I greatly regret that I have set up Saul as king, for he has turned back from following Me, and has not performed My commandments."* *And it grieved Samuel, and he cried out to the Lord all night. So when Samuel rose early in the morning to meet Saul, it was told Samuel, saying, "Saul went to Carmel, and indeed, he set up a monument for himself; and he has gone on around, passed by, and gone down to Gilgal. Then Samuel went to Saul, and Saul said to him, "Blessed are you of the Lord! I have performed the commandment of the Lord. But Samuel said, "What then is this bleating of the sheep in my ears, and the lowing of the oxen which I hear? And Saul said, "They have brought them from the Amalekites; for the people spared the best of the sheep and the oxen, to sacrifice to the Lord your God; and the rest we have utterly destroyed. Then Samuel said to Saul, "Be quiet! And I will tell you what the Lord said to me last night." And he said to him, "Speak on." So Samuel said, "When you were little in your own eyes, were you not head of the tribes of Israel? And did not the Lord anoint you king over Israel? Now the Lord sent you on a mission, and said, 'Go, and utterly destroy the sinners, the Amalekites, and fight against them until they are consumed.' Why then did you not obey the voice of the Lord? Why did you swoop down on the spoil, and do evil in the sight of the Lord? And Saul said to Samuel, But, I have obeyed the voice of the Lord, and gone on the mission on which the Lord sent me, and brought back Agag king of Amalek; I have utterly destroyed the Amalekites. But the people took of the plunder, sheep and oxen, the best of the things which should have been utterly destroyed, to sacrifice to the Lord your God in Gilgal. So Samuel said: Has the Lord as great delight in burnt offerings and sacrifices, As in obeying the voice of the Lord? Behold, to obey is better than sacrifice, And to heed than the fat of rams. For rebellion is as the sin of witchcraft, And stubbornness is as iniquity and idolatry. Because you have rejected the word of the Lord, He also has rejected you from being king. Then Saul said to Samuel, I have sinned, for I have transgressed the commandment of the Lord and your words, because I feared the people and obeyed their voice. Now therefore, please pardon my sin, and return with me, that I may worship the Lord. But Samuel said to Saul, I will not return with you, for you have rejected the word of the Lord, and the Lord has rejected you from being king over Israel. And as Samuel turned around to go away, Saul seized the edge of his robe, and it tore. So Samuel said to him, "The Lord has torn the kingdom of Israel from you today, and has given it to a neighbor of yours, who is better than you". And also the Strength of Israel will not lie nor relent. For He is not a man, that He should relent. Then he said, "I have sinned; yet honor me now, please, before the elders of my people and before Israel, and return with me, that I* may worship the Lord your God. So Samuel turned back after Saul, and Saul worshiped the Lord. Then Samuel said, "Bring Agag king of the Amalekites here to me." So Agag came to him cautiously. And Agag said, "Surely the bitterness of death is past." But Samuel said, "As your sword has made women childless, so shall your mother be childless among women." And Samuel hacked Agag in pieces before the Lord in Gilgal. Then Samuel went to Ramah, and Saul went up to his house at Gibeah of Saul. And Samuel went no more to see Saul until the day of his death. Nevertheless Samuel mourned for Saul, and the Lord regretted that He had made Saul king over Israel." (1 Samuel 15:10-35)

This history is part of the heart of the book of Esther. Haman is introduced in Esther 3. He is the son of Hammedatha. Hammedatha is an Agagite. The story of Esther, which is a beautiful narrative, presents the hatred that is in existence today for the people of God, the nation of Israel! Haman, a hater of God's people wants annihilation of the Jews in Persia. Now it isn't just a nation attacking the rear and killing the defenseless. The enemy is no longer Agag, it is a new generation. The enemy is now led by Haman. Now, it is the entire nation of Israel that is at stake! The heart of the book of Esther is this background. Esther and Mordecai must accomplish what Saul did not.

A second question is this. Who is the unnamed God?

Who is this God?

The Theme of this volume is "God is always at work even when you do not know it!" The question that is obvious is, "who is this God?"

Questions abound about God. Who is He? What does He look like? Where does He live? How can someone talk to God? If there is a God why does He allow suffering? Questions, questions, questions about God!

The Scriptures list numerous names for God. These names help us to understand God. They help us to understand His person and what He is doing!

One of the common names for God is Elohim. It is a name that references God as a magistrate. It is a word of plurality that pictures the almighty as supreme. The first five chapters of Genesis describes God as Elohim. *"In the beginning God created the heavens and the earth. The earth was without form, and void; and darkness was on the face of the deep. And the Spirit of God was hovering over the face of the waters. Then God said, "Let there be light"; and there was light. And God saw the light that it was good; and God divided the light from the darkness." (Genesis 1:1-4)* Genesis 2:4 declares *"This is the history of the heavens and the earth when they were created, in the day that the Lord God made the earth and the heavens."* (Genesis 2:4) The word used for Lord is Jehovah. Jehovah is the Jewish national name for God. The word means the self-existent God!

The terms Elah, Alla, and El speak of God.

In the New Covenant the common term for God is Theos. The definition is a magistrate, the supreme divinity or the exceeding God. In Genesis 1:26 God is seen as plural by the word "us". God is revealed in Scripture in three persons. The Father is God. *"In the beginning God created the heavens and the earth."* (Genesis 1:1) The Son is God. Thomas said so! *"And Thomas answered and said to Him, "My Lord and my God!""* (John 20:28) God the Father said so! *"But to the Son He says: "Your throne, O God, is forever and ever; a scepter of righteousness is the scepter of Your Kingdom."* (Hebrews 1:8) Mary, the mother of our Lord, declares that the baby in her womb is God! *"And my spirit has rejoiced in God my Savior."* (Luke 1:47) The Holy Spirit is God! *"But Peter said, "Ananias, why has Satan filled your heart to lie to the Holy Spirit and keep back part of the price of the land for yourself? "While it remained, was it not your own? And after it was sold, was it not in your own control? Why have you conceived this thing in your heart? You have not lied to men but to God."* (Acts 5:3,4) Peter tells Ananias that he lied to God and clearly identifies the Holy Spirit as God.

The theme of the Scripture is the glory of God. The glory of God refers to the splendor and honor of God! The book of Esther never mentions God. Yet the book is full of God's presence. It is this writers' contention that although the book is accurately named Esther, the book is about this marvelous God. As we journey through life God is always at work even when we do not know it.

This thought of God leads us to the third question which is . . .

What is the Value of the Book of Esther?

The book of Esther is often accompanied with great reviews. "Esther has often been described as a "master of literature" (Stirred, "Bushes Esther pp.107-8) and "a literacy treasure" (Kaiser, pp. 198) even by secular literacy standards. Such high praise is given by those who do not highly regard its historicity. It has been described as a historical romance (Gunkel), an ethical legend, a historical novel (Berg, pg.14; Moore, Esther, pg. 111). It has been submitted to careful literacy analysis by technical experts (C.G. Berg, Bommershaosen), but its literacy merits and readability are apparent even to the untrained. The plot is skillfully narrated with a paucity of word and swiftly carries the reader along with its climatic denoucement."(1) In the book there is the hero, Mordecai; the heroine Esther, the villain, Haman; two potential assassins, Bigtha and Teresh plus a sensual, self-centered king. With ten words the author unravels a story that details the characters. There is contrast, surprise, heartache, glimpses of humor, hyperbole, and frankly very few difficult passages. The Apocrypha joins in. In the Apocrypha there are "The Additions to the Book of Esther." Much has been written and speculation is vast of this book. To the Jewish family it is a victory. To the Gentile world it is a book of intrigue.

The book shows how God rules and overrules. Some volumes spend lengthy discussions on apparent historical inaccuracies. For example the book opens describing 122 provinces. Historical evidence seems to point to somewhere around 20 to 29 provinces. It is interesting to note that Darius divided the kingdom into satraps. The Hebrew word in Esther 1:1 could actually be rendered province. This can be understood to be an administrative subdivision of a satrap.

Another apparent historical inaccuracy is the name of the king. His name is, however, consistent with historical writers such as Herodotus.

There are answers critical for all the apparent discrepancies. The fast moving events bring us back to the theme of this book. Despite the king and Haman's plans the unnamed God was directing everything. This God was also able to overrule the retributive law of the land, the law of the Medes and Persians.

Perhaps the greatest literacy value of the book is that even though a people can be far from God, they are still in His heart and His protective care.

Although God's name is not mentioned and the king's name is mentioned 29 times this is a theological masterpiece with great emphasis on the Jewish people. Where is the kingdom of the Medes-Persians today? Where are the nations of many Old Testament peoples"? Vanished. The Jewish people continue to journey back to Israel! Interesting. Now to the location of the story –

Where did this Happen?

The opening of the book of Esther describes the place that the story of Esther and the Jews took place. *"In those days when King Ahasuerus sat on the throne of his kingdom, which was in Shushan the citadel,"* (Esther 1:2) Cyrus the Great passed on to the Persian Empire various customs. Susa was an ancient city. It was the background of Elamite, Persian, and Parthian empires of Iran. This is the location where Daniel the prophet lived. Cyrus named three capitals of the Persian Empire. Shushan is the Hebrew form of Susa.

The area today is modern Iran. Archeology has discovered numerous ornaments in this region. An image that was unearthed was an image of a soldier depicting the "immortal guards" who were in charge of protecting the monarch.

This location is east of the famous Tigris River (about 150 miles). The name is taken from a water lily that apparently grew in lakes and swamps and other waterways.

Some years ago my wife and I visited the Louvre Museum in Paris, France. We saw there a part of the remains of Susa with an inscription from king Darius which said "This palace which I built at Susa."

The events at this location took place during the Babylonian captivity. Solomon's temple was destroyed by the Babylonians. The Jews were taken into exile. All the Jews did not live here. They were scattered all over various provinces of the empire. Some Jews during the Persian Captivity were allowed to go back to Jerusalem. Mordecai, while raising his young cousin was a man of authority and decided to stay in Shushan. Decisions lead to destinations. His destination would put him in a position so that Esther could deliver the people of God.

CHAPTER ONE

THE DISMISSAL OF THE QUEEN

N ow let's dive into the story about the God who is always at work. Chapter 1 opens with the dismissal of Queen Vashti. She is thrown out of the kingdom. This sets the stage for the exaltation of Esther, who, in chapter 2, is put in a position to become queen.

"Now it came to pass in the days of Ahasuerus, (this is Ahasuerus which reigned, from India even unto Ethiopia, over an hundred and seven and twenty provinces:) That in those days, when the king Ahasuerus sat on the throne of his kingdom, which was in Shushan the palace, In the third year of his reign, he made a feast unto all his princes and his servants; the power of Persia and Media, the nobles and princes of the provinces, being before him: When he shewed the riches of his glorious kingdom and the honour of his excellent majesty many days, even an hundred and fourscore days." (Esther 1:1-4)

The king has at least three names. His Persian name is spelled *Khshayershan*. The king's Hebrew name is *Ahasuerus*. His Greek name is *Xerxes*. His father was Darius and his grandfather was Cyrus the Great.

He reigned for 21 years, from 486 to 465 B.C. In this time the land was divided into districts and provinces with mayors and governors. The king was in charge. In the United States of America citizens are free to elect our leaders and then replace them during the next election, but in Persia the king was the absolute ruler. In England there is a queen. She reigns but does not rule. Parliament rules. In Persia the king reigned and ruled.

Verses 5-9 addresses the king's **pride**. Eastern kings loved to host banquets, and there are three banquets in chapter 1 alone. In the first four verses Ahasuerus hosts the key political and military leaders of the land. Later there is a feast in the winter palace at Shushan, and finally there is an event involving Vashti and the women of Shushan.

Eastern leaders were men of huge egos and lavish plans. In this instance the king did not bring all of the leaders together at one time. To do that would cause these leaders to be absent from their responsibilities in the government. Probably these leaders came to Shushan on a rotating schedule. It is also probable that they all gathered together at the week-long activity.

"And when these days were expired, the king made a feast unto all the people that were present in Shushan the palace, both unto great and small, seven days, in the court of the garden of the king's palace; Where were white, green, and blue, hangings, fastened with cords of fine linen and purple to silver rings and pillars of marble: the beds were of gold and silver, upon a pavement of red, and blue, and white, and black, marble. And they gave them drink in vessels of gold, (the vessels being diverse one from another,) and royal wine in abundance, according to the state of the king. And the drinking was according to the law; none did compel: for so the king had appointed to all the officers of his house, that, they should do according to every man's pleasure. Also Vashti the queen made a feast for the women in the royal house which belonged to king Ahasuerus." (Esther 1:5-9)

The rulers of the Eastern World in this time of history enjoyed hosting huge, lavish banquets. The purpose was to impress the guests with the success of the ruler and his kingdom. Power, wealth, and authority were the signature of the monarchs. Ahasuerus was like so many leaders. He was a proud man and enjoyed flaunting his lifestyle and empire. People who are privileged to be in authority need to keep in mind that all power comes from God. *"Let every soul be subject to the governing authorities.*

For there is no authority except from God, and the authorities that exist are appointed by God." (Romans 13:1) God is in complete control over all the issues of life. King Herod Agrippa I is a prime example of pride leading to destruction. *"Now Herod had been very angry with the people of Tyre and Sidon; but they came to him with one accord, and having made Blastus the king's personal aide their friend, they asked for peace, because their country was supplied with food by the king's country. So on a set day Herod, arrayed in royal apparel, sat on his throne and gave an oration to them. And the people kept shouting, "The voice of a god and not of a man!" Then immediately an angel of the Lord struck him, because he did not give glory to God. And he was eaten by worms and died."* (Acts 12:20-23) The story of men like Herod and Ahasuerus lead to the heartache of many followers who are affected by the heartless leadership but also their hopeless end.

There are six other banquets found in the book of Esther. A feast for Esther is cited in Esther 2:18 and Haman hosts an event for the king in Esther 3:15. Chapters 5 and 7 detail two banquets organized by Esther for Haman, and these are crucial to the entire story.

In Esther 8:17, we read, *"And in every province and city, wherever the king's command and decree came, the Jews had joy and gladness, a feast and a holiday. Then many of the people of the land became Jews, because fear of the Jews fell upon them."* This was essentially a holiday, and often in this era a holiday meant a temporary suspension of taxes. I know many people, especially in my home state of New York, who would welcome a day or two of that. Another feast is mentioned in chapter 9, illustrating once again how important these events were to life in Persia and in the king's circle.

It is important to consider the history of the region at this time. Bible teacher, Warren Wiersbe in his discussion on Esther, refers to the writings of the historian Heroditus indicating ongoing discussions between Ahasuerus and his leaders regarding the invasion of Greece. His father was defeated at Marathon in 490 B.C. and the son wanted revenge. He wanted, in the words of Heroditus, to "reduce the whole earth into one empire." (2) There were a number of such men throughout that period of history, such as Alexander the Great, who not only wanted authority over a specific country but set out to rule the known world. That was the attitude of Ahasuerus.

It was also common at this time for a king to invite both dignitaries and commoners to the palace to impress them with the trappings of the throne, from the marble pillars to the gold-trimmed drapes and table service. Kings desired everyone to think highly of them. Ahasuerus was no different. It is interesting to note that history records the destruction of the Persian army in 480 B.C., bringing his dream of world conquest to an end.

As Scripture states, *"Pride goes before destruction, and a haughty spirit before a fall."* (Proverbs 16:18) History teaches us about Pharoah, Nebuchadnezzar, Belshazzar, Sennacherib, and Herod. More recent history gives us such examples as Hitler and Bin Laden. Each of these men were consumed by a huge ego, and that is what we see in the first nine verses of Esther 1. Pride leads to downfall.

From the beginning of history God has an intended role for men and women. In our spiritual condition we are His special vessels. Spiritually, when one trusts Christ, male and female are one in Christ. The roles of men and women are provided throughout Scripture. Many women are strong leaders. Esther is an example. In the home God has ordained men to be the spiritual leaders as Christ is the head of the church. Jesus loved the church and sacrificed Himself for the church and describes His role as loving the bride of Christ as His own body. Men are men and women are women. The misuse of women has been an age long problem. Here in the Persian Empire it was obvious that women were considered less in importance than men. God never ordained nor planned it that way. Often the lack of love and commitment by men promotes the misuse and mistreatment of women. Ahasuerus was an example of narcissism and male domination that has no place in a government or home. His attitude was one that was typical of eastern monarchs. Control, a super ego, and fleshly desires permeated his outlook. He became childish, immature, and when he filled himself with strong drink he went to extreme by asking his wife to display her beautiful body before the inebriated leaders.

We notice the king's **problem** in verses 10-12. *"On the seventh day, when the heart of the king was merry with wine, he commanded Mehuman, Biztha, Harbona, Bigtha, and Abagtha, Zethar, and Carcas, the seven chamberlains that served in the presence of Ahasuerus the king, To bring Vashti the queen before the king with the crown royal, to shew the people and the princes her beauty: for she was fair to look on. But the queen Vashti refused to come at the king's commandment by his chamberlains: therefore was the king very wroth, and his anger burned in him." (Esther 1:10-12)*

Verse 10 points out that the king was very drunk. Although the king desired to control all things, he could not control himself. People begin to act differently when they consume excess amounts of alcohol. He wanted his queen to come out and parade before the guests so they could be as impressed with her as they were with his other possessions. That is how he looked at Vashti. He may have intended for her to display her naked body for all to see.

But she said no. Wiersbe summarizes the entire first chapter with the phrase, "When the queen said no." A large number of men in today's society think they have control of their wives, while most of those same wives disagree (and they are probably correct). In Persia at this time, however, a woman did not challenge a man. To make matters worse, Vashti was disobeying her husband, and the problem added a third layer when one considers that she was in defiance of the king.

Ahasuerus, in his drunken state and being accustomed to having everyone around him catering to his every whim, misses an important principle: all authority comes from God.

In the time of Moses with his leadership over the children of Israel, one can see that God was emphatic about avoiding strong drink. Look at Deuteronomy 29:5-6. *"And I have led you forty years in the wilderness: your clothes are not waxen old upon you, and thy shoe is not waxen old upon thy foot. Ye have not eaten bread, neither have ye drunk wine or strong drink: that ye might know that I am the LORD your God."* In Leviticus 10:8-11, the priests were ordered not to drink strong wine. There are other specific references to drinking throughout the Bible. A Chinese proverb says, "*A man takes a drink, and the drink takes the man.*" (3) That is exactly what happened to Ahasuerus in the first chapter of Esther.

What a horrendous misuse of a woman. The king wants his queen to do something indecent, but she wants to do what is right. He is only concerned with his position and the prestige it affords. His counselors tell him, "If you let her get away with this, it won't be long before every woman in the kingdom thinks she can act this way." That wasn't true but they convinced him it was. The problem, however, was obvious. If he could not control his wife, how could he command the Persian armies?

"*There is neither Jew nor Greek, there is neither bond nor free, there is neither male nor female: for ye are all one in Christ Jesus.*" (Galatians 3:28) What a beautiful statement regarding the position of men and women. Our rights are based upon the gospel of Christ, but Ahasuerus did not look at his wife that way at all. To him, she was a possession he could use to promote his godlessness and his pride.

In Esther 1:13-22 we have what I like to call the **proclamation**, in which the king decides what he thinks he must do. Francis Bacon once wrote, "A man who studies revenge keeps his own wounds green which otherwise would heal and do well." Revenge in the heart of a man is not a good thing, but that is what the king had in mind.

"*Then the king said to the wise men who understood the times (for this was the king's manner toward all who knew law and justice, those closest to him being Carshena, Shethar, Admatha, Tarshish, Meres, Marsena, and Memucan, the seven princes of Persia and Media, who had access to the king's presence, and who ranked highest in the kingdom): "What shall we do to Queen Vashti, according to law, because she did not obey the command of King Ahasuerus brought to her by the eunuchs?" And Memucan answered before the king and the princes: "Queen Vashti has not only wronged the king, but also all the princes, and all the people who are in all the provinces of King Ahasuerus. For the queen's behavior will become known to all women, so that they will despise their husbands in their eyes, when they report, 'King Ahasuerus commanded Queen Vashti to be brought in before him, but she did not come.' This very day the noble ladies of Persia and Media will say to all the king's officials that they have heard of the behavior of the queen. Thus there will be excessive contempt and wrath.* (Esther 1:13-18)

The king's counselors, who studied the stars as astrologers were to help with their efforts to advise him, and make their case that the queen had to go. Her behavior simply could not be tolerated in the kingdom.

The king's attitude here is best summarized in Proverbs 12:16. *"A fool's wrath is known at once, but a prudent man covers shame."* If he had formulated a plan and taken some time to consider his course of action, it would have been much better. Instead, he made a rash decision based upon his desire to teach everyone in the kingdom, especially the women, a lesson.

A good question for lengthy discussion and assessment is "what causes someone to follow a leader?" The seven "wise" counsellors gave followship but not counsel! Their encouragement is that all the men in the kingdom should act like the king. Is it possible that the dictatorial commands of a brutal leader can promote qualities of followship? Are hearts truly changed and different because of the decrees of a government? Would such a wicked decree by this king promote women to have love for their husbands? The counsel and advice from sacred scripture is quite different. *"And do not be drunk with wine, in which is dissipation; but be filled with the Spirit, speaking to one another in psalms and hymns and spiritual songs, singing and making melody in your heart to the Lord, giving thanks always for all things to God the Father in the name of our Lord Jesus Christ, submitting to one another in the fear of God. Wives, submit to your own husbands, as to the Lord. For the husband is head of the wife, as also Christ is head of the church; and He is the Savior of the body. Therefore, just as the church is subject to Christ, so let the wives be to their own husbands in everything. Husbands, love your wives, just as Christ also loved the church and gave Himself for her, that He might sanctify and cleanse her with the washing of water by the word, that He might present her to Himself a glorious church, not having spot or wrinkle or any such thing, but that she should be holy and without blemish. So husbands ought to love their own wives as their own bodies; he who loves his wife loves himself. For no one ever hated his own flesh, but nourishes and cherishes it, just as the Lord does the church. For we are members of His body, of His flesh and of His bones. "For this reason a man shall leave his father and mother and be joined to his wife, and the two shall become one flesh." This is a great mystery, but I speak concerning Christ and the church. Nevertheless let each one of you in particular so love his own wife as himself, and let the wife see that she respects her husband."* (Ephesians 5:18-33)

On a personal note, God has allowed me (at this writing) to be in leadership for nearly one half a century. I am still learning and have much to learn. One thing I do know is that those whom God gives me the privilege to lead need my respect and compassion as well as firm direction. None of this attitude is seen in the king's leadership.

Now notice the king's decision:

"If it pleases the king, let a royal decree go out from him, and let it be recorded in the laws of the Persians and the Medes, so that it will not be altered, that Vashti shall come no more before King Ahasuerus; and let the king give her royal position to another who is better than she. When the king's decree which he will make is proclaimed throughout all his empire (for it is great), all wives will honor their husbands, both great and small." (Esther 1:19-20)

At the end of verse 20 is the mindset of the king's advisors: "We'll show those women who is in charge."

The king agreed. *"And the reply pleased the king and the princes, and the king did according to the word of Memucan. Then he sent letters to all the king's provinces, to each province in its own script, and to every people in their own language, that each man should be master in his own house, and speak in the language of his own people."* (Esther 1:21-22)

We do not know for certain, but it would be interesting to know what ultimately happened to Vashti. Some Bible historians believe that she became the mother of Artaxerxes, who reigned after Ahasuerus. If that was the case, then she did quite well for herself. The fact that Ahasuerus eventually lost his kingdom and his life can serve as a reminder to us that our sin will always find us out (Num. 32:23). You cannot run from God, because He is always there.

CHAPTER TWO

A QUEEN CHOSEN

A s we turn to the second chapter of Esther, consider these words written by A.B. Simpson: "God is preparing His heroes, and when the opportunity comes He can fit them into their places in a moment, and the world will know they are there but will not know where they came from."(4) That, is exactly what happened in this story with a young girl named Esther.

When one thinks of great men and women of the Old Testament – Ezekiel, Daniel, Isaiah, and Ruth, just to name a few – it is interesting to note how they appeared to simply burst on the scene, but God was always preparing them.

Based on calls we have received at Davis College a number of churches are looking for pastors. It can be a great struggle to find the right pastor for a church, however, I, believe that, somewhere, God is preparing the man for the place.

When we talk about marriage, we tell young people, "God has someone for you." I met my wife when we were students at the same college where I am now president, and my youth pastor told me, "Always pray that God will lead you to the right person." I thought that was great advice, but I became bolder and asked the Lord, "Please let me know what she looks like, so when she comes by I'll know it's her."

A young lady walked into class one day, and I thought to myself, "She is the one." I even told her that, but she didn't believe me. It took me a while to convince her, but at this writing, we have been married nearly 47 years.

With Vashti out of the picture, there had to be a replacement. God was already preparing someone. At the same time, a plan was being formed to eliminate the Jewish people. God has always had a special place for the Jews. We receive His Word through the Jewish people. The Messiah came through Jewish lineage. God was not about to let His plan for the Jews be derailed.

As time passed, the king began to regret his decision regarding Vashti, so he began **the search** for a new queen. Notice the first four verses of chapter 2. *"After these things, when the wrath of King Ahasuerus subsided, he remembered Vashti, what she had done, and what had been decreed against her. Then the king's servants who attended him said: "Let beautiful young virgins be sought for the king; and let the king appoint officers in all the provinces of his kingdom, that they may gather all the beautiful young virgins to Shushan the citadel, into the women's quarters, under the custody of Hegai the king's eunuch, custodian of the women. And let beauty preparations be given them. Then let the young woman who pleases the king be queen instead of Vashti. This thing pleased the king, and he did so."*

It appears that a beauty contest was organized, and it is likely that at least some of the women involved were not too thrilled with it. The king probably had a fling with several of the young ladies of his choosing before deciding on the winner. I think that if I were a parent at this time I would never want something like this to happen to my daughter, and I imagine many parents in the kingdom felt the same way.

In Esther 2: 5-18 we see **the selection** of the new queen, and through this passage we are introduced to Mordecai, who will become a key figure in the story. Mordecai is mentioned 58 times in the book of Esther, and seven times he is referred to as a Jew, beginning with verses 5-7. *"In Shushan the citadel there was a certain Jew whose name was Mordecai the son of Jair, the son of Shimei, the son of Kish, a Benjamite. Kish had been carried away from Jerusalem with the captives who had been captured with Jeconiah king of Judah, whom Nebuchadnezzar the king of Babylon* *had carried away. And Mordecai had brought up Hadassah, that is, Esther, his uncle's daughter, for she had neither father nor mother. The young woman was lovely and beautiful. When her father and mother died, Mordecai took her as his own daughter."* In six other places in Esther (5:13, 6:10, 8:7, 9:29, 9:31, 10:3) this man is called simply *"Mordecai the Jew."* *"Yet all this avails me nothing, so long as I see Mordecai the Jew sitting at the king's gate."* (Esther 5:13) *"Then the king said to Haman, "Hurry, take the robe and the horse, as you have suggested, and do so for Mordecai the Jew who sits within the king's gate! Leave nothing undone of all that you have spoken."* (Esther 6:10) *"Then King Ahasuerus said to Queen Esther and Mordecai the Jew, "Indeed, I have given Esther the house of Haman, and they have hanged him on the gallows because he tried to lay his hand on the Jews."* (Esther 8:7) *"Then Queen Esther, the daughter of Abihail, with Mordecai the Jew, wrote with full authority to confirm this second letter about Purim."* (Esther 9:29) *"to confirm these days of Purim at their appointed time, as Mordecai the Jew and Queen Esther had prescribed for them, and as they had decreed for themselves and their descendants concerning matters of their fasting and lamenting."* (Esther 9:31) *"For Mordecai the Jew was second to King Ahasuerus, and was great among the Jews and well received by the multitude of his brethren, seeking the good of his people and speaking peace to all his countrymen."* (Esther 10:3)

There is something very important to understand about Mordecai. His lineage is outlined in verse 5, specifically that he is a descendant of Kish of the tribe of Benjamin. His ancestors were taken to Babylon from Jerusalem when Cyrus was king of Persia. About 50,000 Jews were given the privilege of returning to Jerusalem. Some of them did not return. Mordecai was one of those who stayed in Persia, and we will see later in the story, the reason. One of the reasons Haman had so much hatred for Mordecai was his lineage, he was a descendant of Kish.

As the opening of this book points out there was bitter antagonism with the descendants from Agag. It appears that Mordecai knows the story of Saul, Agag, and the Amalekites, Haman's hatred was based on his knowledge of Mordecai's lineage.

In verse 7, Esther is introduced. Her Jewish name was Hadassah, which is an interesting word that means "myrtle." Esther is her Persian name and it refers to a star. The myrtle tree is actually a flower that looks like a star. So now we have two Jewish people in fairly prominent positions in the Persian government.

America was founded on Christian principles. But when a nation begins to move away from God, the populous begins to think less about the things of God – even those who have been followers of God. Could this be true of Esther and Mordecai?

It is normal to think that Mordecai and Esther, as Jewish people in the Persian Empire, would have maintained a kosher home and followed Jewish customs so that anyone who saw them would know they are Jews. Amazingly, however, no one in the palace at this time knows that they are Jewish. Matthew Henry once said, "All truths are not to be spoken of at all times."(5) The Jewish nation was backslidden at this time, although we should not judge Mordecai and Esther too harshly in that regard. There is no evidence that they attempted to keep their lineage a secret while Esther was growing up, yet others simply did not know it.

We then see the **encouragement of Hegai**, who supervised the harem, *"So it was, when the king's command and decree were heard, and when many young women were gathered at Shushan the citadel, under the custody of Hegai, that Esther also was taken to the king's palace, into the care of Hegai the custodian of the women. Now the young woman pleased him, and she obtained his favor; so he readily gave beauty preparations to her, besides her allowance. Then seven choice maidservants were provided for her from the king's palace, and he moved her and her maidservants to the best place in the house of the women."* (Esther 2:8-9)

How fascinating it is that God worked through this man and his harem. God can work through the heart, soul, and mind of a keeper of the harem. Hegai was a Gentile. He gave the women a beauty treatment that included dietary guidelines, perfume, and cosmetics. They were prepared in this way so they could satisfy the king, but Esther received special treatment among these women through the providence of God. Seven choice maidservants were provided for Esther from the king's palace.

"Esther had not revealed her people or family, for Mordecai had charged her not to reveal it. And every day Mordecai paced in front of the court of the women's quarters, to learn of Esther's welfare and what was happening to her." (Esther 2:10-11)

Business and political decisions were made at the gate to the city. The area around the gate was the location of all of the governmental activities. This was where Mordecai placed himself each day, watching for any sign of what might be happening with Esther and wondering what God might have in store for them.

Acts 15:18 says, *"Known to God from eternity are all His works."* We should never think that God is not at work. In this story, while much of the nation is permeated with a hatred for the Jewish people, the queen is a Jew!

Some versions of the Bible note that the king loved Esther, but perhaps it was more like a simple physical attraction. The king's approval comes in verses 12-*18 "Each young woman's turn came to go in to King Ahasuerus after she had completed twelve months' preparation, according to the regulations for the women, for thus were the days of their preparation apportioned: six months with oil of myrrh, and six months with perfumes and preparations for beautifying women. Thus prepared, each young woman went to the king, and she was given whatever she desired to take with her from the women's quarters to the king's palace. In the evening she went, and in the morning she returned to the second house of the women, to the custody of Shaashgaz, the king's eunuch who kept the concubines. She would not go in to the king again unless the king delighted in her and called for her by name. Now when the turn came for Esther the daughter of Abihail the uncle of Mordecai, who had taken her as his daughter, to go in to the king, she requested nothing but what Hegai the king's eunuch, the custodian of the women, advised. And Esther obtained favor in the sight of all who saw her. So Esther was taken to King Ahasuerus, into his royal palace, in the tenth month, which is the month of Tebeth, in the seventh year of his reign. The king loved Esther more than all the other women, and she obtained grace and favor in his sight more than all the virgins; so he set the royal crown upon her head and made her queen instead of Vashti. Then the king made a great feast, the Feast of Esther, for all his officials and servants; and he proclaimed a holiday in the provinces and gave gifts according to the generosity of a king."* (Esther 2:12-18)

A new maiden was brought to the king each night. The following morning she was sent back to the house of the concubines. In most cases it was a one night stand. The king most likely lost track of the individuality of this parade of young women. This is lust at its peak. Indulgence does not satisfy.

When Esther came before the king she came with the reference of everyone's favor. The words, "The king loved Esther" in the King James Version appears to mean that he was attracted to her.

So the king chose Esther. Typically, the king orders a great banquet. He proclaims a national holiday. Gifts are given to the people. The king desires that everyone is to feel good about the new queen. God is not mentioned. Yet by the providence of God a Jewish woman is placed into the Persian Kingdom next to the king!

There was a certain beauty and flair about Hadassah. We see in verse 15 that everyone who saw Esther said, "That is the queen." She was accepted! God allowed this to happen, even with unbelieving people. We should never limit the power of God in whatever He is about to do.

Notice in verses 19-23 of chapter 2 an interesting intervention that takes place. *"When virgins were gathered together a second time, Mordecai sat within the king's gate. Now Esther had not revealed her family and her people, just as Mordecai had charged her, for Esther obeyed the command of Mordecai as when she was brought up by him. In those days, while Mordecai sat within the king's gate, two of the king's eunuchs, Bigtha and Teresh, doorkeepers, became furious and sought to lay hands on King Ahasuerus. So the matter became known to Mordecai, who told Queen Esther, and Esther informed the king in Mordecai's name. And when an inquiry was made into the matter, it was confirmed, and both were hanged on a gallows; and it was written in the book of the chronicles in the presence of the king."* (Esther 2:19-23)

The second "gathering of the virgins" in verse 19 is a glimpse into the king's heart. He will continue having physical relationships with the virgins. Esther would not be his "one and only!" The king chose to bring into his bed chamber the beautiful virgins of the harem. Although the Scripture does not describe the attitude of the women, there must have been a hatred by the virgins recognizing their purity was stolen by this egomaniac.

It is interesting to note that Mordecai is at the king's gate. This is the position of the privileged few. Perhaps Esther used her influence to get Mordecai, her cousin, the position. Only a handful of individuals had access to the king.

Two men, Bigtha and Teresh attempt to kill the king. We are not really told why these men acted the way they did, but for some reason they wanted to kill the king. Perhaps they had someone they preferred to be queen. The one who warned the king about the plot was none other than Mordecai. He received no reward for that, but the incident was recorded as we read in verse 23, and later through the providence of God he received the recognition he deserved.

The events in this story are a constant reminder of the promise contained in Prov. 13:21. *"Evil pursueth sinners: but to the righteous good shall be repaid."* Do the right thing, and it will come back around.

Let's consider four lessons we can glean from the story so far:

Character precedes desire. This king lived his life solely for what he wanted, but there is so much more to life than that.

Love is an intimate relationship. It is nefarious to truly find love in the process this king used.

National corruption often begins with leaders. Americans should always pray that the right leaders are elected in our country, and once they are in office we must continue to pray for them.

Religion is boring, but Christianity is enlightening. God works in our lives and causes miraculous things to take place, just as He did for Esther.

Much of the story of Esther is concerned with the lineage of the Jewish people. Throughout history we have seen repeated attempts to do away with the Jews because they are the people from whom we received the Messiah, the King of Kings and Lord of Lords. But when God starts to do something, there is no one who can stop it. We must have confidence in that.

CHAPTER THREE

THE VILLAN

There is peace in the land. *Ahasuerus,* is king. Esther is the queen. Mordecai is busy with the business at the king's gate. A villain is introduced. His name is Haman. Historically, he is so vilified by Jewish people that at the Feast of Purim when the book of Esther is read publically in Jewish synagogues, whenever Haman's name is mentioned the congregants stamp their feet shouting 'may his name be blotted out!' Haman is the one individual among many who exemplifies the hatred of the Jewish people. He is the one amongst many remembered for trying to exterminate the Jewish population.

Haman is a dangerous man. He represents the genealogy of a people who historically have been in direct opposition to God. In the opening of this book this author presented the story of the king of the Amalekites, Agag. God had declared war on the Amalekites. This wicked nation attacked the woman and children at the rear of the marching nation.

"Now Amalek came and fought with Israel in Rephidim. And Moses said to Joshua, "Choose us some men and go out, fight with Amalek. Tomorrow I will stand on the top of the hill with the rod of God in my hand." So Joshua did as Moses said to him, and fought with Amalek. And Moses, Aaron, and Hur went up to the top of the hill. And so it was, when Moses held up his hand, that Israel prevailed; and when he let down his hand, Amalek prevailed. But

Moses' hands became heavy; so they took a stone and put it under him, and he sat on it. And Aaron and Hur supported his hands, one on one side, and the other on the other side; and his hands were steady until the going down of the sun. So Joshua defeated Amalek and his people with the edge of the sword. Then the Lord said to Moses, "Write this for a memorial in the book and recount it in the hearing of Joshua, that I will utterly blot out the remembrance of Amalek from under heaven." And Moses built an altar and called its name, The-Lord-Is-My-Banner." (Exodus 17:8-15)

Additionally, Moses told Joshua to fight against Amalek. Joshua won. God also stated that this nation was to be wiped off the face of the earth. When the Israelites were to enter the Promised Land, God reminded them of the wickedness of the Amalekites.

"Remember what Amalek did to you on the way as you were coming out of Egypt, How he met you on the way and attacked your rear ranks, all the stragglers at your rear, when you were tired and weary; and he did not fear God. Therefore it shall be, when the Lord your God has given you rest from your enemies all around, in the land which the Lord your God is giving you to possess as an inheritance, that you will blot out the remembrance of Amalek from under heaven. You shall not forget." (Deuteronomy 25:17-19)

As the opening of this book reminded readers, the first king of Israel, Saul, failed. He did not obey the Lord. He allowed the Amalekites to live. Haman is now one of their descendants. Saul was a Benjamite. He failed. Mordecai was a Benjamite. He now would take up the battle. The founder of the Amalekites was Esau. *Thus we have*:

Haman's Background

There is nothing good about Haman. I have ministered at hundreds of funerals. I can say that I never was faced with a situation where there was "nothing good to say" about someone. With Haman there is nothing good to say! He is a wicked man with wicked plans coming from a wicked heart. He is a hater of Israel's God. From this background we notice:

His Boasting

"After these things King Ahasuerus promoted Haman, the son of Hammedatha the Agagite, and advanced him and set his seat above all the princes who were with him." (Esther 3:1)

Over a five year period the king decided to make Haman the equivalent of a chief operating officer. Haman takes a position of authority. From a casual observation this appears to be a major injustice. The theme of this book is one of life's major lessons. God is always at work even when we do not know it. Haman, is the epitome of pride. Arrogance takes charge under a gullible king.

Authority often reveals what is in someone's heart. A good leader desires to do what is best for others. Haman is the opposite of Godly leadership.

We now are introduced to:

His Blight

"And all the king's servants who were within the king's gate bowed and paid homage to Haman, for so the king had commanded concerning him. But Mordecai would not bow or pay homage. ³ Then the king's servants who were within the king's gate said to Mordecai, "Why do you transgress the king's command?" ⁴ Now it happened, when they spoke to him daily and he would not listen to them, that they told it to Haman, to see whether Mordecai's words would stand; for Mordecai had told them that he was a Jew. ⁵ When Haman saw that Mordecai did not bow or pay him homage, Haman was filled with wrath. ⁶ But he disdained to lay hands on Mordecai alone, for they had told him of the people of Mordecai. Instead, Haman sought to destroy all the Jews who were throughout the whole kingdom of Ahasuerus—the people of Mordecai." (Esther 3:2-6)

Haman loved the spotlight. Public recognition was his forte. Fearing that people would not bow to him, Haman coerces the king to give an edict that demanded everyone bow to him. Perhaps others in the kingdom felt that Haman received his position through coercion: Therefore he was to have a public recognition through the king's edict. "When little men cast long shadows, it is a sign the sun is setting."(6)

Mordecai refused to bow to Haman. Evidently, Mordecai understands the history and genealogy of this wicked chief operating officer. It is not wrong to bow to people. Believers in Scripture bowed. Joseph's brothers bowed to their brother, the prime minister. *"Now Joseph was governor over the land; and it was he who sold to all the people of the land. And Joseph's brothers came and bowed down before him with their faces to the earth."* (Genesis 42:6) The Jews bow to each other. *"And Ahimaaz called out and said to the king, "All is well!" Then he bowed down with his face to the earth before the king, and said, "Blessed be the Lord your God, who has delivered up the men who raised their hand against my lord the king!"* (II Samuel 18:28) Mordecai will not bow as it would demonstrate allegiance to a false deity.

Mordecai has gone public. He is a Jew. Haman now looks for him. His anger is boiling to a steady rage. He personally hates Mordecai and all that he represents. Mordecai's refusal to bow is not personal but based on principle.

The destruction of the Jews has been the Satanic desire. The Messiah would come of Jewish lineage.

There are some occasions in Scripture when believers practice civil disobedience. This is one of those occurrences. *"We ought to obey God rather than men"*. (Acts 5:29) Daniel and his friends would not eat the king's food (Daniel 1). The apostles were put in prison (Acts 16). In each case the Lord's followers were doing what was right with a heart of respect for their leadership. There needs to be Biblical conviction that directs an individual.

Mordecai takes his stand. Haman's hatred continues to grow. Haman plots to not only rid himself of Mordecai, but the entire Jewish population.

THE PLOT THICKENS

"In the first month, which is the month of Nisan, in the twelfth year of King Ahasuerus, they cast Pur (that is, the lot), before Haman to determine the day and the month, until it fell on the twelfth month, which is the month of Adar. Then Haman said to King Ahasuerus, "There is a certain people scattered and dispersed among the people in all the provinces of your kingdom; their laws are different from all other people's, and they do not keep the king's laws. Therefore it is not fitting for the king to let them remain. If it pleases the king, let a decree be written that they be destroyed, and I will pay ten thousand talents of silver into the hands of those who do the work, to bring it into the king's treasuries." So the king took his signet ring from his hand and gave it to Haman, the son of Hammedatha the Agagite, the enemy of the Jews. And the king said to Haman, "The money and the people are given to you, to do with them as seems good to you." Then the king's scribes were called on the thirteenth day of the first month, and a decree was written according to all that Haman commanded—to the king's satraps, to the governors who were over each province, to the officials of all people, to every province according to its script, and to every people in their language. In the name of King Ahasuerus it was written, and sealed with the king's signet ring. And the letters were sent by couriers into all the king's provinces, to destroy, to kill, and to annihilate all the Jews, both young and old, little children and women, in one day, on the thirteenth day of the twelfth month, which is the month of Adar, and to plunder their possessions. A copy of the document was to be issued as law in every province, being published for all people, that they should be ready for that day. The couriers went out, hastened by the king's command; and the decree was proclaimed in Shushan the citadel. So the king and Haman sat down to drink, but the city of Shushan was perplexed." (Esther 3:7-15)

Haman begins to accelerate the plot. He and the astrologers select a day. A private meeting is held. The false deities are consulted. The stars and galaxies with accompanying omens were sought. Purim, meaning lot, is a Babylonian word that means the casting of lots. With purpose, Haman begins the event of Nisan. This is the month the Jews celebrate the Passover, the deliverance from Egypt. Haman's anger appears vengeful and vitriolic. The date is set. The thirteenth day of the twelfth month! (v. 13) This providentially would give Mordecai and Esther time. One year is a long time. Haman's hatred would grow. Revenge would be sweet. He probably dreamed of seeing the Jews in panic and distress. Mordecai, however, would have time to prepare. God is at work!

Haman approaches the king. His description is vague. He mentions that their laws are different. He exaggerates Mordecai's disobedience. He portrays all the people as disobedient to the king and his empire.

All despots fear an overthrow of their government. Haman portrays the worst case of civil disobedience. He then put the proverbial icing on the cake. He offers 10,000 talents of silver to the king. Warren Wiersbe points out from the Greek historian, Herodotus, that the annual income of the entire Persian Empire was 15,000 talents of silver. (7) Haman's offer is 2/3's of the yearly income. It is correct to assume that Haman was wealthy but also that he would take the possessions of the Jews. He would eventually take the Jewish wealth. The king's response was typical of monarchs in this day. In essence he said 'keep the money,' yet he would expect Haman to come through with the gift.

The royal signet ring was the seal of the king. It was the most important authority symbol of the king. With it any documents could be rendered under the authority of the Medes and Persians. The king gives Haman the ring.

As the Jews prepare for their beloved feast Haman writes a new law. Haman's plan is to destroy the Jews and take their possessions. It is interesting to note the similarity to God's edict to Saul in I Samuel 15:1-3 " *Samuel also said to Saul, 'The Lord sent me to anoint you king over His people, over Israel. Now therefore, heed the voice of the words of the Lord. Thus says the Lord of hosts: 'I will punish Amalek for what he did to Israel, how he ambushed him on the way when he came up from Egypt. Now go and attack Amalek, and utterly destroy all that they have, and do not spare them. But kill both man and woman, infant and nursing child, ox and sheep, camel and donkey.'* " The only difference is that Saul was not to keep the Amalekites possessions and that the possessions of the Jews were to be taken by the Amalekite's eventual son – Haman! The document is written. The couriers set out to distribute it. Once the law is written, it is final. The law of the Medes and Persians cannot be rescinded. The plan works!

The plan is literally the annihilation of the Jewish people. All looks good! Haman has won! Or, has he? The fact is this....in three months he will be a dead man!

CHAPTER FOUR

A SERIOUS SITUATION

W̲e see this scoundrel Haman. We come to Esther 4 and see the Jewish people in a serious situation. Verses 1-4 show us **Mordecai's expression**.

"When Mordecai learned all that had happened, he tore his clothes and put on sackcloth and ashes, and went out into the midst of the city. He cried out with a loud and bitter cry. He went as far as the front of the king's gate, for no one might enter the king's gate clothed with sackcloth. And in every province where the king's command and decree arrived, there was great mourning among the Jews, with fasting, weeping, and wailing; and many lay in sackcloth and ashes. So Esther's maids and eunuchs came and told her, and the queen was deeply distressed. Then she sent garments to clothe Mordecai and take his sackcloth away from him, but he would not accept them. (Esther 4:1-4)

While this was happening, Haman was with the king having a drink and a great time in the palace. We can infer from verse 1 that Mordecai was crying out to God, but words like "prayer" and references to the Lord are absent from the book of Esther. Also, wearing sackcloth near the palace was highly unusual because the king wanted to maintain a "no worries" image of fun and merriment.

Mordecai feared greatly what might happen to his people, and when Esther sent him clothes to wear, he refused them because he was making a statement. He longed for someone to step up and help his people. The situation brings to mind the famous words of Burke: "All that is required for evil to triumph is for good men to do nothing."

Mordecai expresses courage. He was a Jew. He went public that he was a Jew. He opposed the edict. Human lives, thousands of them, are at risk. It is time for someone to take a stand. Mordecai with deep conviction did.

The king's image must be one of an artificial portrayal that all was fine. Sackcloth was not acceptable.

Word arrives to the Queen. She sends Mordecai some new garments. He refuses to take them. He is making a clear statement about the crisis at hand.

Mordecai is not only fearing his own life. He fears for the lives of others.

Mordecai's explanation is shown in verses 5-9 of Esther 4. *"Then Esther called Hathach, one of the king's eunuchs whom he had appointed to attend her, and she gave him a command concerning Mordecai, to learn what and why this was. So Hathach went out to Mordecai in the city square that was in front of the king's gate. And Mordecai told him all that had happened to him, and the sum of money that Haman had promised to pay into the king's treasuries to destroy the Jews. He also gave him a copy of the written decree for their destruction, which was given at Shushan, that he might show it to Esther and explain it to her, and that he might command her to go in to the king to make supplication to him and plead before him for her people. So Hathach returned and told Esther the words of Mordecai."*

A eunuch named Hathach plays a key role in this phase of the story. I am always amazed by the people who appear in the pages of God's Word, some named and some unnamed, who are greatly used by God. One obvious example would be the lad who brought his lunch to a gathering with Jesus and saw Him feed five thousand with it. Another is the young maid who brought about the healing of Naaman because she had knowledge of the prophet Elisha. These instances serve to remind us that, no matter how small we think our role might be, if God is in it we can accomplish much.

It is very important to understand what Mordecai is teaching us here. If we refuse to obey God, then He could take responsibility and privilege meant for us and give it to someone else. This happened to John Mark in the New Testament when God used Timothy. On the other hand, He could discipline us like He did with Jonah to emphasize what we are supposed to do. No matter what happens, God is always on time. Imagine that you are boarding a ship bound for Europe. You may do many different things on board as a passenger, but that ship is going to Europe regardless of what you are doing. I am convinced that if Mordecai and Esther had not been obedient in this story, God would still have accomplished His plan.

Mordecai has a copy of the decree. Additionally he has a copy for Esther to read. He is evidently in a high position of government. His access to the queen is not only because of lineage but also because of position. If you, dear reader, have position and privilege, it would be wise to examine what you can accomplish for God's kingdom. Mordecai desires that Esther reveal her national identity.

Mordecai tells Hathach to explain to the queen his need for mercy. He tells Hathach that he is a Jew and Esther is a Jewess.

In verses 10-17 of Esther 4, we see **Mordecai's exhortation**. *"Then Esther spoke to Hathach, and gave him a command for Mordecai: "All the king's servants and the people of the king's provinces know that any man or woman who goes into the inner court to the king, who has not been called, he has but one law: put all to death, except the one to whom the king holds out the golden scepter, that he may live. Yet I myself have not been called to go in to the king these thirty days." So they told Mordecai Esther's words. And Mordecai told them to answer Esther: "Do not think in your heart that you will escape in the king's palace any more than all the other Jews. For if you remain completely silent at this time, relief and deliverance will arise for the Jews from another place, but you and your father's house will perish. Yet who knows whether you have come to the kingdom for such a time as this?" Then Esther told* *them to reply to Mordecai: "Go, gather all the Jews who are present in Shushan, and fast for me; neither eat nor drink for three days, night or day. My maids and I will fast likewise. And so I will go to the king, which is against the law; and if I perish, I perish!" So Mordecai went his way and did according to all that Esther commanded him."*

Esther feared that she could be killed for simply entering the king's presence, which would accomplish nothing. Mordecai reminded her that if she did nothing, eventually she would go down with the rest of the Jews. She began to realize that God wanted to do something great here and He wanted to use her to do it.

A.B. Simpson wrote, "In the moral conflict raging around us, whoever is on God's side is on the winning side and cannot lose. Whoever is on the other side is on the losing side and cannot win."

Jeremiah 29:11 says, *"For I know the thoughts that I think toward you, saith the LORD, thoughts of peace, and not of evil, to give you an expected end."* "To give you an expected end" can also be translated as *"a future and a hope."* Our future is as bright as the promise of God, which is that one day we will be with Him forever. But He has a purpose for us now as well.

Esther received a challenge in verse 14, as Mordecai told her she was in that place at that time for a reason. Her choice would determine her legacy for generations. Amazing! We are still talking about her more than three thousand years later.

What is God's intention for you right now in your life? Think about it. Why does God have you in the place you are at this moment? It is not by chance. God has a purpose for you.

When I was a pastor I frequently visited a dear lady who could not get out of bed. She lay on her back for 14 years before she died, and I never knew her when she was not in this condition. Usually she was more of an encouragement to me than I was to her, and she told me, "I live to encourage those who come to visit me." She felt that was her purpose.

Recently I spoke to a pastor in his mid-60s and asked him how much longer he expected to be in the pastorate. "I have a greater vision now than I have ever had in my life," he said.

God has all of us here for such a time as this. If you are alive today, God is not finished with you. We need to step up by faith and do what He has for us to do. The devil likes to give us just enough trouble to stop us in our tracks, but that is the best time to take a step of faith.

Look verses 15-17 of Esther 4 and see Mordecai's expediting the plan. *"Then Esther told them to reply to Mordecai: "Go, gather all the Jews who are present in Shushan, and fast for me; neither eat nor drink for three days, night or day. My maids and I will fast likewise. And so I will go to the king, which is against the law; and if I perish, I perish!" So Mordecai went his way and did according to all that Esther commanded him."*

It is good to fast in certain situations if your health permits such an activity. A Christian will often fast and pray to seek the will of God in a particular time of need. Esther did that here as she considered a potentially life-threatening move for herself as well as her people. The king was known as someone whose emotions resembled a roller coaster. Many of us know people in our lives that we treat with care, seeking the appropriate time to discuss certain things in fear of how they might react. Esther knew she could have met with the same fate as Vashti, but she was willing to take the risk. She purposed to do whatever it took to get the job done, and that is a major step in any person's life.

Their backs were against the wall. The future of the Messiah's legacy and genealogy was at stake. But we must remember that had they not been obedient, God would have raised up another Esther and another Mordecai to see that His work was done.

I believe that God first anoints a person, not a movement or a ministry. When a person is anointed, then the ministry can be anointed, and ultimately God builds a monument to His glory. Pride cannot be a part of that process.

God raised up Esther, a Jewish woman in the Persian Empire, to be the queen. God went on to use Mordecai, who could have gone back to his homeland but chose to stay in the Persian Empire, to encourage Esther to stand fast and do what God would have her do.

The law was against Esther, the government was against her, her gender was against her – it seemed as though everything was stacked up against her. But Rom. 8:31 says, *"If God be for us, who can be against us?"*

The promises of God are always the same, even when we do not understand how He is at work. Look at Psalms 7:14-17 *"Behold, the wicked brings forth iniquity; yes, he conceives trouble and brings forth falsehood. He made a pit and dug it out, and has fallen into the ditch which he made. His trouble shall return upon his own head, and his violent dealing shall come down on his own crown. I will praise the LORD according to His righteousness, and will sing praise to the name of the LORD Most High."*

Friedrich von Logau wrote a poem entitled "Retribution." Here is what he wrote:

Though the mills of God grind slowly,

Yet they grind exceeding small;

Though with patience he stands waiting,

With exactness grinds he all.(8)

Two statements, (in the form of a question) in this passage are the most famous from the book of Esther. In Mordecai's pleading with Esther he asks *"…Yet who knows whether you have come to the kingdom for such a time as this"* (verse 14). God has Esther in this position for a purpose. It is wise to think through God's place for you in His kingdom. The second is Esther's response. The famous words are, *"Go, gather all the Jews who are present in Shushan, and fast for me; neither eat nor drink for three days, night or day. My maids and I will fast likewise. And so I will go to the king, which is against the law; and if I perish, I perish!"* The words… "if I perish, I perish"… (Esther 4:16) are the heart of Esther's story. She was taking her stand with her people. She was also in the flow of God's purpose for her. This unnamed God had a major task for her.

It is interesting to note the call to fast. Fasting and prayer are often placed together in Scripture. This fasting is not a religious nor disciplinary exercise. For many years, I fasted one day a week but often it was for discipline. I did it for health reasons. This fasting was for humility, brokenness, introspection, and a major request. The Jews were fasting in the kingdom (Esther 4:3). The Gentile women who surrounded Esther would continue to fast and pray. For the Jews this was now a matter of life and death.

CHAPTER FIVE

THE UNNAMED GOD AT WORK

Esther 5 is part of the section of the story that shows God's **divine sovereignty**. Look at the first five verses:

"Now it happened on the third day that Esther put on her royal robes and stood in the inner court of the king's palace, across from the king's house, while the king sat on his royal throne in the royal house, facing the entrance of the house. So it was, when the king saw Queen Esther standing in the court, that, she found favor in his sight, and the king held out to Esther the golden scepter that was in his hand. Then Esther went near and touched the top of the scepter. And the king said to her, "What do you wish, Queen Esther? What is your request? It shall be given to you—up to half the kingdom!" So Esther answered, "If it pleases the king, let the king and Haman come today to the banquet that I have prepared for him." Then the king said, "Bring Haman quickly, that he may do as Esther has said." So the king and Haman went to the banquet that Esther had prepared." (Esther 5:1-5)

Esther put on her royal robes for this occasion with great fear. She knew it could be her final day. But the king was glad to see her, and she was accepted into his presence. He was ready to give her just about anything she might ask for.

There are some things about Jewish law and customs that Esther knew very well. She was well aware of God's directive to Abram in Gen. 12:1-3. *"Now the Lord had said to Abram: "Get out of your country, from your family and from your father's house, to a land that I will show you. I will make you a great nation; I will bless you and make your name great; and you shall be a blessing. I will bless those who bless you, and I will curse him who curses you; and in you all the families of the earth shall be blessed."*

Some of the covenants in the Bible are conditional. The Abrahamic Covenant, however, was unconditional. Study the life of Abram and you will see that while it was a life of faith, he fumbled the ball a few times along the way. But God did what he promised to do, which was to make him great and a blessing.

Was Abram great? We are still talking about him after thousands of years. Was he a blessing? Through him and his lineage we have the Word of God and the Messiah. Two nations come from his loins.

God told Abram that other people would be blessed or cursed depending upon how they treated him and his people and perhaps Esther remembered this unconditional promise of God, and that allowed her to approach the king with boldness. Our only source of boldness for living the Christian life is from Christ and the Word of God.

When Solomon built the temple and dedicated it, he gave a small speech and a long prayer. He asked the Lord about the future and what would happen if the people strayed from Him. This is recorded in II Chronicles 6.

After the dedication in the opening verses of II Chronicles 7, God's response is seen in verses 13-14. *"When I shut up heaven and there is no rain, or command the locusts to devour the land, or send pestilence among My people, if My people who are called by My name will humble themselves, and pray and seek My face, and turn from their wicked ways, then I will hear from heaven, and will forgive their sin and heal their land."* That last verse is often quoted when discussing the future of the United States of America; our problems do not start in Washington or the state capital, but with us as God's people.

Esther made it into the king's presence and found favor with him. This was possibly because she remembered the Abrahamic covenant, but also because the Jewish people had been fasting and praying. Their backs were against the wall, and they needed God to do something.

Esther invited Ahasuerus and Haman to a banquet, knowing that both of them loved that kind of event. When the king asked his queen what she desired, she gave a brilliant response that could only have come from God. It is contained in verses 6-8. *"At the banquet of wine the king said to Esther, "What is your petition? It shall be granted you. What is your request, up to half the kingdom? It shall be done!" Then Esther answered and said, "My petition and request is this: If I have found favor in the sight of the king, and if it pleases the king to grant my petition and fulfill my request, then let the king and Haman come to the banquet which I will prepare for them, and tomorrow I will do as the king has said."* (Esther 5:6-8)

Haman was loving this. He knew he had the king on his side, and now he was thinking that the queen was on his side as well. What he did not know was that Esther had not revealed everything she knew. Perhaps she realized that it was not yet the right time or the right place. Maybe she wanted to catch Haman off guard.

I've participated in debates and one of the goals of a debater is to catch the opponent off guard. If you did that, people would think you knew what you were talking about.

A few years ago we threw a birthday party for my son who lived in New Jersey at our house in New York. I was supposed to keep him away from the house for a few hours to set up the surprise, but I didn't know my wife had invited a number of people to a birthday party for me! Since our birthdays are close together, I thought it was for him. I pulled into the driveway and thought nothing of the many cars parked at our house, and I was still clueless when I walked in the door and everyone yelled, "Surprise!" I thought it was for my son, but it was for me! My wife had pulled one over on me!

In a more serious setting Esther was working hard to keep Haman a step behind. He was a very wicked man who suspected nothing as he drank liquor with the king and plotted the death of fifteen million Jews. The queen fasted and prayed, and she had a plan that was divinely appointed.

A powerful message can be found in Proverbs 16:1. *"The preparations of the heart belong to man, but the answer of the tongue is from the Lord."* Notice also Proverbs 19:21. *"There are many plans in a man's heart, Nevertheless the Lord's counsel— that will stand."* As Haman schemed to bring about the demise of God's chosen people, God made certain that His plan was accomplished instead.

The **fallacy of the man** known as Haman is seen in full view in verse 9 of the fifth chapter of Esther. *"So Haman went out that day joyful and with a glad heart; but when Haman saw Mordecai in the king's gate, and that he did not stand or tremble before him, he was filled with indignation against Mordecai."* The arrogance and wickedness in Haman's heart was amazing.

Imagine Haman's feeling of exhilaration. He meets with the king and queen! Haman and the two leaders! What an honor. Haman was exhilarated! The king and Haman had a close relationship and now he had the same with the queen! It is fascinating to see the queen's plan in front of an overconfident Haman who viewed his future with a false confidence. Little did he know his days were numbered!

He went home and told his family and friends how great things were going in verses 10-13. *"Nevertheless Haman refrained himself: and when he came home, he sent and called for his friends, and Zeresh his wife. And Haman told them of the glory of his riches, and the multitude of his children, and all the things wherein the king had promoted him, and how he had advanced him above the princes and servants of the king. Haman said moreover, Yea, Esther the queen did let no man come in with the king unto the banquet that she had prepared but myself; and tomorrow am I invited unto her also with the king. Yet all this availeth me nothing, so long as I see Mordecai the Jew sitting at the king's gate."* (Esther 5:10-13)

He had all of these riches and so much power, but he let the very sight of Mordecai ruin all of that. Fortunately for him (he thought), his wife came up with a plan of her own in verse 14. *"Then his wife Zeresh and all his friends said to him, "Let a gallows be made, fifty cubits high, and in the morning suggest to the king that Mordecai be hanged on it; then go merrily with the king to the banquet." And the thing pleased Haman; so he had the gallows made."* (Esther 5:14) Haman had filled his wife and friend's mind with a hatred of Mordecai and the Jews. Haman takes his wife's suggestion and builds gallows seventy-five feet high. The plan was clear. Mordecai would be hung in sight of the Jews. The Jews would be convinced that the king was serious and the law was irreversible.

Persians were known for impaling live prisoners on sharp posts and leaving them there to die vicious deaths. Little did Haman realize he built the very gallows he would soon be executed on.

There are some things to remember as we conclude this chapter. As Esther realized with Mordecai's help that she was in her important position for a purpose, each of us should seek God and discover what He wants for us in our own lives. If you are discouraged about the direction of your life, remember that God has a plan for you just as He did for Esther. Sometimes it requires a step of faith, but God has something great in store.

Do you think the prayers of the Jewish people had an impact on the heathen king? I believe that the Lord changes events and circumstances when His people pray. What a great God we serve.

As we finish Esther 5, Haman was on top of the world. In chapter 6, his world started crashing down.

CHAPTER SIX

A 24 HOUR REVERSAL

♔

The changes came rather quickly. This chapter details a 24-hour period of time. Verses 1-5 take place in the evening, verses 6-10 the following morning, and verses 11-14 that afternoon.

There are parallels to Esther in the "wisdom books" of the Bible and it would be good for us to see one of those. The example is found in Ecclesiastes 5:12. "*The sleep of a laboring man is sweet, whether he eat little or much: but the abundance of the rich will not suffer him to sleep.*" What an interesting thought. Sometimes the rich and powerful have so much on their minds that it makes rest difficult, and Esther 6 opens with the king finding himself in a similar situation.

Notice verses 1-3. "*That night the king could not sleep. So one was commanded to bring the book of the records of the chronicles; and they were read before the king. And it was found written that Mordecai had told of Bigthana and Teresh, two of the king's eunuchs, the doorkeepers who had sought to lay hands on King Ahasuerus. Then the king said, "What honor or dignity has been bestowed on Mordecai for this?" And the king's servants who attended him said, "Nothing has been done for him."*" (Esther 6:1-3)

Ahasuerus had all of the women and entertainment one could imagine at his disposal, but when he was unable to sleep he asked for the Chronicles to be read. That would be like one of us getting out the dictionary to read when we can't sleep. Nothing against the dictionary but it does not make entertaining reading.

He was reminded of Mordecai's heroics in Esther 2, when he warned of an assassination plot that saved the king's life. At this point Ahasuerus discovered that Mordecai had never been honored for his good deed, and he set about changing that beginning in verses 4-5. *"So the king said, "Who is in the court?" Now Haman had just entered the outer court of the king's palace to suggest that the king hang Mordecai on the gallows that he had prepared for him. The king's servants said to him, "Haman is there, standing in the court." And the king said, "Let him come in."* (Esther 6:4-5)

Normally there was no one lingering in the court without a specific reason. While these verses do not say so, it is not unreasonable to assume that Haman may have set his sights on the throne by this time, as he thought all of his plans were working so beautifully. That attitude is found often in our society. I have a friend who owned a booming business that sent him all over the country, and one day he told me of a group of employees in one location that tried to take over his business. That story, the height of disloyalty, is very common.

Haman did not know it at the time, but his presence in the court was not due to his own cunning but because God wanted him there at the king's disposal.

Perhaps the greatest Christian philosopher of the twentieth century was C.S. Lewis. By chance he read a book by MacDonald that led to his faith in Christ. Wally Beebe, who was renowned across the nation for teaching churches how to effectively use the bus ministry in the latter half of the twentieth century, came to Christ after finding a gospel tract lying in a restroom stall. These types of incidents seem to come about by chance, but we know that God lets nothing happen by chance.

We never know what God is about to do. Here was this wicked, prideful, arrogant king who could not sleep. He made a decision regarding Mordecai, and Haman just happened to be nearby. It was all because God was at work.

Look at Psalm 33:10-11. *"The Lord brings the counsel of the nations to nothing; He makes the plans of the peoples of no effect.*

The counsel of the Lord stands forever, the plans of His heart to all generations." Haman had what he thought was a brilliant plan that could not possibly fail, but this passage tells us that his plan was changed by the unnamed God!

The morning's events began to unfold in verse 6. *"So Haman came in, and the king asked him, "What shall be done for the man whom the king delights to honor?" Now Haman thought in his heart, "Whom would the king delight to honor more than me?"* (Esther 6:6) Haman had no idea of the surprise that awaited him.

Look at verses 7-9. *"And Haman answered the king, "For the man whom the king delights to honor, let a royal robe be brought which the king has worn, and a horse on which the king has ridden, which has a royal crest placed on its head. Then let this robe and horse be delivered to the hand of one of the king's most noble princes, that he may array the man whom the king delights to honor. Then parade him on horseback through the city square, and proclaim before him: 'Thus shall it be done to the man whom the king delights to honor!'* (Esther 6:7-9)

This kind of treatment was always reserved for royalty. Haman was convinced that the king meant to honor him this way, coming prior to Mordecai and the rest of the Jewish people's annihilation. Imaging his shock at hearing the king's words in verse 10. *"Then the king said to Haman, "Hurry, take the robe and the horse, as you have suggested, and do so for Mordecai the Jew who sits within the king's gate! Leave nothing undone of all that you have spoken."* (Esther 6:10)

This must have seemed like a knife in the back. Even if this honor were not intended for Haman himself, he would have wanted someone other than Mordecai to receive it.

It is important at this time to recall Mordecai's challenge to Esther in chapter 4 and her crucial decision about whether to stand up for her people. She was risking instant death for herself, but now God was turning the tide in her favor.

You can imagine how the Jews in Persia absolutely hated Haman. He certainly knew this, which made it even more humiliating for him to lead the procession of the man he hated most on a parade of highest honor through the city.

"So Haman took the robe and the horse, arrayed Mordecai and led him on horseback through the city square, and proclaimed before him, "Thus shall it be done to the man whom the king delights to honor!" Afterward Mordecai went back to the king's gate. But Haman hurried to his house, mourning and with his head covered. When Haman told his wife Zeresh and all his friends every-thing that had happened to him, his wise men and his wife Zeresh said to him, "If Mordecai, before whom you have begun to fall, is of Jewish descent, you will not prevail against him but will surely fall before him. While they were still talking with him, the king's eunuchs came, and hastened to bring Haman to the banquet which Esther had prepared." (Esther 6:11-14)

God often delays something. If Mordecai had been rewarded five years prior to this event the story would be different. God's timing was perfect. The system of punishment and rewards in the Persian Empire were common. How did Mordecai's good deed go unrewarded? God did this! God's in charge of plans, programs, systems, schedules, and events. We should plan and schedule as best we can but often God is the one who changes it as He wishes. A delay by God is purposeful. It may not be a denial but timing is everything.

Haman is up through the night, probably enjoying the con-struction of the gallows. Haman is there on time. Ahasueras reads the Chronicles to him. God's plan, as always, is not just timely but it is perfect.

When Haman was invited into the room for the banquet he thought this was the ultimate honor only it became the first step to his tragic end.

How quickly things had changed. Just a day after dining with the king and basking in the glow of his status, Haman was embar-rassed and in mourning. His wife, who had encouraged him so much with her idea of the gallows for Mordecai, now tells him he is doomed. Before she could get the words out of her mouth, Haman was called to Esther's banquet. He didn't even have time to think.

This leads us to chapter 7, where Ahasuerus and Haman arrived to dine with Esther. For her this was a divine appointment, the culmination of a plan orchestrated by God.

CHAPTER SEVEN

A PERFECT PLAN

Have you ever wondered why certain things happen that seem destined to end badly? According to Ecclesiastes. 8:11, *"Because the sentence against an evil work is not executed speedily, therefore the heart of the sons of men is fully set in them to do evil."* People often continue to do evil because they think they are getting away with it, but God will never be mocked. Your sin will always find you out.

Look at the **request of the queen** in the first four verses of Esther 7. *"So the king and Haman went to dine with Queen Esther. And on the second day, at the banquet of wine, the king again said to Esther, "What is your petition, Queen Esther? It shall be granted you. And what is your request, up to half the kingdom? It shall be done!" Then Queen Esther answered and said, "If I have found favor in your sight, O king, and if it pleases the king, let my life be given me at my petition, and my people at my request. For we have been sold, my people and I, to be destroyed, to be killed, and to be annihilated. Had we been sold as male and female slaves, I would have held my tongue, although the enemy could never compensate for the king's loss."* (Esther 7:1-4)

Even the wording of her request showed the great wisdom Esther received from God. She almost made it sound as if the king's own reputation depended upon how he responded.

The most important phrase in this passage is at the end of verse 3, where Esther referred to *"my petition, and **my** people at my request."* This is where she admitted that she was a Jew, just before she revealed the plot to wipe out her people.

The king is drinking. The king's offer to Esther is more than generous. Most scholars teach that when a monarch used the term "...even to half the kingdom" it was not to be taken literally but it was a generous offer. It is like an American saying "....half of the world." In other words "tell me what you want and I will do my best."

I imagine Esther's heart was pounding. Her future and those of her people are at stake. Haman must have been devastated to find that Esther is a Jew. In glowing terms she honors the king. She wants to please him. Our approach to those in authority should always be of respect for the position. As she unfolds the issue the king realizes he has ordered the death, not just of Mordecai and the Jews but also the queen! She makes it clear that murder of the whole group cannot be ignored!

This revelation brought about the **rage of the king** in verses 5-8. *"So King Ahasuerus answered and said to Queen Esther, "Who is he, and where is he, who would dare presume in his heart to do such a thing?" And Esther said, "The adversary and enemy is this wicked Haman!" So Haman was terrified before the king and queen. Then the king arose in his wrath from the banquet of wine and went into the palace garden; but Haman stood before Queen Esther, pleading for his life, for he saw that evil was determined against him by the king. When the king returned from the palace garden to the place of the banquet of wine, Haman had fallen across the couch where Esther was. Then the king said, "Will he also assault the queen while I am in the house?" As the word left the king's mouth, they covered Haman's face."* (Esther 7:5-8)

The king learned that his most trusted advisor was plotting behind his back. I have learned over the years in my ministry to be careful whom I trust. Think about whom you have chosen to be your confidantes – those you believe in, who believe in you, that you can sit and talk with openly and honestly about the important things in life.

Haman was put into his position quickly, and there is no evidence of anything he did to deserve it except that it was the king's desire. If anyone, it should have been Mordecai in the lofty post because of how he saved Ahasuerus' life.

Imagine how Haman felt when Esther identified him as the perpetrator of this horrific plot. He was already hurt by having the king order him to put Mordecai on the royal horse and parade him through the city. Now he was in fear of his own life, while the proud king felt as though he had been made a fool by the doings of his right-hand man.

There is a great warning for all of us in Proverbs 18:13. *"He who answers a matter before he hears it, It is folly and shame to him."* The king acted impulsively throughout his reign, thinking it was his right to do as he pleased, and that landed him squarely in this situation he now faced.

Simply put, Haman was a tool of the devil, who since the time of Abraham has wanted to destroy the Jewish people. After being furious over a Jewish man's refusal to bow before him, he now found himself prostrate before a Jewish woman as he begged for his life.

Haman's pleas were so emotional and impassioned that he fell across Esther's couch, and when the king returned from the garden it appeared that Haman was trying to assault the queen. That brought about the **reward of Haman** in verses 9-10.

"Now Harbonah, one of the eunuchs, said to the king, "Look! The gallows, fifty cubits high, which Haman made for Mordecai, who spoke good on the king's behalf, is standing at the house of Haman." Then the king said, "Hang him on it!" So they hanged Haman on the gallows that he had prepared for Mordecai. Then the king's wrath subsided." (Esther 7:9-10)

Talk about a tough day. Talk about a turnaround. The fall of Haman was complete.

However, the decree was still in place. Once a law of the Medes and the Persians was enacted, that was that. It was a done deal. Even the king could not change it. He could put out another decree to counteract it, but he could not change it.

So the Jews were now subject to attack by the Persians, and since the kingdom consisted of a hundred million people, the Jews were a relatively small minority.

CHAPTER EIGHT

VICTORY!

ote in the first two verses of Esther 8 the **promotion of Mordecai**. *"On that day King Ahasuerus gave Queen Esther the house of Haman, the enemy of the Jews. And Mordecai came before the king, for Esther had told how he was related to her. So the king took off his signet ring, which he had taken from Haman, and gave it to Mordecai; and Esther appointed Mordecai over the house of Haman."* (Esther 8:1-2) The king was still quick to give his signet ring to someone, as he had done with Haman. This time, though, he was attempting to erase any evidence of Haman's existence from the kingdom.

Read verse 15. *"So Mordecai went out from the presence of the king in royal apparel of blue and white, with a great crown of gold and a garment of fine linen and purple; and the city of Shushan rejoiced and was glad."* (Esther 8:15) What a day for this faithful servant of God.

There are people in the world today who possess an intense hatred of the Jews. Mahmoud Ahmadinejad, a recent leader of Iran, denied the Holocaust and called for the elimination of the nation of Israel, or having it "wiped off the map," as some claim he said. I can tell you today that it will never happen, because the Lord will not allow it.

But our faith in the United States of America is under attack as well. Some of our own political leaders like to talk about freedom of worship. We believe we have freedom of religion, which is something totally different. Freedom of worship means you can go into a church building but not take your faith outside that building. We believe in taking the gospel to people, which a lot of Americans do not want us to do, so in some ways we need wisdom like Esther. There will always be persecution against the Jews and against the people of God, but if He could deliver Esther and Mordecai in such a bizarre story that does not even mention His name, I imagine He can look out for us also.

Verses 3-6 contain the **petition of Esther**. *"Now Esther spoke again to the king, fell down at his feet, and implored him with tears to counteract the evil of Haman the Agagite, and the scheme which he had devised against the Jews. And the king held out the golden scepter toward Esther. So Esther arose and stood before the king, and said, "If it pleases the king, and if I have found favor in his sight and the thing seems right to the king and I am pleasing in his eyes, let it be written to revoke the letters devised by Haman, the son of Hammedatha the Agagite, which he wrote to annihilate the Jews who are in all the king's provinces. For how can I endure to see the evil that will come to my people? Or how can I endure to see the destruction of my countrymen?"* (Esther 8:3-6) Haman was gone, but the edict was still in place.

Haman is dead! The decree lives. The law of the Medes and Persians cannot be altered. The Persians with their millions would attack the 15 million Jews and they would be annihilated. Don't forget; this is the story of the unnamed God who is always at work.

"On that day King Ahasuerus gave Queen Esther the house of Haman, the enemy of the Jews. And Mordecai came before the king, for Esther had told how he was related to her. So the king took off his signet ring, which he had taken from Haman, and gave it to Mordecai; and Esther appointed Mordecai over the house of Haman." (Esther 8:1-2)

Haman's property equally belonged to king Ahasuerus. The king chose to give it to Esther. You as the reader can decide whether this was an act of generosity or one of atoning for the king's reputation. Esther gives the gift to the trusted Mordecai.

The most important issue is that the signet ring once given to Haman (Esther 3:10) is now given to Mordecai. In the Persian Empire there is now a Jewish queen and Jewish Chief Operating Officer.

Mordecai is dressed in the specular garb of a Persian leader. The borrowed robes and garments of fasting are laid aside. The blue and brilliant white with a turban is placed on Mordecai. *"So Mordecai went out from the presence of the king in royal apparel of blue and white, with a great crown of gold and a garment of fine linen and purple; and the city of Shushan rejoiced and was glad.* (Esther 8:15)

Esther again petitions the king. *"Now Esther spoke again to the king, fell down at his feet, and implored him with tears to counteract the evil of Haman the Agagite, and the scheme which he had devised against the Jews. And the king held out the golden scepter toward Esther. So Esther arose and stood before the king, and said, "If it pleases the king, and if I have found favor in his sight and the thing seems right to the king and I am pleasing in his eyes, let it be written to revoke the letters devised by Haman, the son of Hammedatha the Agagite, which he wrote to annihilate the Jews who are in all the king's provinces. For how can I endure to see the evil that will come to my people? Or how can I endure to see the destruction of my countrymen?"* (Esther 8:3-6) Her request is to save the people. *"Pray for the peace of Jerusalem: "May they prosper who love you."* (Psalms 122:6) This is a prayer we regularly need in our lives. Pray for our Jewish friends!

"Then King Ahasuerus said to Queen Esther and Mordecai the Jew, "Indeed, I have given Esther the house of Haman, and they have hanged him on the gallows because he tried to lay his hand on the Jews. You yourselves write a decree concerning the Jews, as you please, in the king's name, and seal it with the king's signet ring; for whatever is written in the king's name and sealed with the king's signet ring no one can revoke." So the king's scribes were called at that time, in the third month, which is the month of Sivan, on the twenty-third day; and it was written, according to all that Mordecai commanded, to the Jews, the satraps, the governors, and the princes of the provinces from India to Ethiopia, one hundred

and twenty-seven provinces in all, to every province in its own script, to every people in their own language, and to the Jews in their own script and language. And he wrote in the name of King Ahasuerus, sealed it with the king's signet ring, and sent letters by couriers on horseback, riding on royal horses bred from swift steeds. By these letters the king permitted the Jews who were in every city to gather together and protect their lives—to destroy, kill, and annihilate all the forces of any people or province that would assault them, both little children and women, and to plunder their possessions, on one day in all the provinces of King Ahasuerus, on the thirteenth day of the twelfth month, which is the month of Adar. A copy of the document was to be issued as a decree in every province and published for all people, so that the Jews would be ready on that day to avenge themselves on their enemies. The couriers who rode on royal horses went out, hastened and pressed on by the king's command. And the decree was issued in Shushan the citadel. So Mordecai went out from the presence of the king in royal apparel of blue and white, with a great crown of gold and a garment of fine linen and purple; and the city of Shushan rejoiced and was glad. The Jews had light and gladness, joy and honor. And in every province and city, wherever the king's command and decree came, the Jews had joy and gladness, a feast and a holiday. Then many of the people of the land became Jews, because fear of the Jews fell upon them." (Esther 8:7-17)

The issue is very clear. How can the war against the Jews be reversed?

The king could not legally change nor revoke the law. But there could be a new law written. Mordecai in his position, could draft a new law, sign it with the signet ring, and he did so. The law stated that the Jews could defend themselves against anyone who tried to harm, kill, or take the property of the Jews. The law would have to be written in a similar fashion to the previous one. A little over two months passed from the previous law written by Haman. In chapter 9 we find the Jews killed only those who attacked them. They killed only the men. *"And in Shushan the citadel the Jews killed and destroyed five hundred men."* And the king said to Queen Esther, *"The Jews have killed and destroyed five hundred men in Shushan the citadel, and the ten sons of Haman. What have they done in the rest of the king's provinces? Now what is your petition? It shall be granted to you. Or what is your further request? It shall be done." And the Jews who were in Shushan gathered together again on the fourteenth day of the month of Adar and killed three hundred men at Shushan; but they did not lay a hand on the plunder."* (Esther 9:6, 12, 15) They did not keep any of the goods. 75,000 were killed out of 100 million. 75,000 men ready to kill defenseless Jews.

God's promise is through the Abrahamic Covenant. *"Now the Lord had said to Abram: "Get out of your country, from your family and from your father's house, to a land that I will show you. I will make you a great nation; I will bless you and make your name great; and you shall be a blessing. I will bless those who bless you, and I will curse him who curses you; and in you all the families of the earth shall be blessed."* (Genesis 12:1-3)

Mordecai writes the edict and sends it out. *"The couriers who rode on royal horses went out, hastened and pressed on by the king's command. And the decree was issued in Shushan the citadel."* (Esther 8:14) The Jews are saved. The chapter begins with the feast of Esther. It ends with the joy and feasting of the nation. Joy and gladness is repeated in verses 15 to 17. Many turned to this nameless God. *"So Mordecai went out from the presence of the king in royal apparel of blue and white, with a great crown of gold and a garment of fine linen and purple; and the city of Shushan rejoiced and was glad. The Jews had light and gladness, joy and honor. And in every province and city, wherever the king's command and decree came, the Jews had joy and gladness, a feast and a holiday. Then many of the people of the land became Jews, because fear of the Jews fell upon them."* (Esther 8:15-17) Gentiles in the Old Testament are turning to the Jewish God. Who could have believed it earlier on in this book?

I've had the privilege to make many trips to the Holy Land, and every time as we leave we are reminded by those who live there of the words of Psalm 122:6, which says, *"Pray for the peace of Jerusalem: "May they prosper who love you."* We know that real and lasting peace will only come when the Prince of Peace returns, but we should still pray for peace in Jerusalem. The Bible teaches us that the land given to Abraham belongs to His people and no one else.

Consider the following lessons from this portion of the book of Esther:

It is obvious that **God has a chosen people who are the apple of his eye**. I imagine He feels about the nation of Israel and the Jewish people the same way I feel about my own grandchildren. They are the best! Similarly, we should not think of ourselves inferior in any way, because we are the people of God.

Always listen to God before listening to men. That is so difficult for us to do at times. Ahasuerus was the kind of guy who liked to do his own thing, and he allowed Haman to have undue influence over him without even realizing it.

God is always at work. This is a recurring theme that we have mentioned often during the study of Esther, but it is so true. Even when we do not see it or understand it, God is always doing something, and His timing is accurate and certain.

Salvation is not based on our works. It is always by grace through faith in Christ.

CHAPTER NINE

A NEW DAY

A new decree was put into place in Esther 9 to allow the Jews to defend themselves against attack. As we noted earlier, the previous decree conceived by Haman could not be taken away, but a new decree could be enacted.

The first 16 verses of chapter 9 describe the **vindication of the Jews**. Look at verses 1-2. *"Now in the twelfth month, that is, the month of Adar, on the thirteenth day, the time came for the king's command and his decree to be executed. On the day that the enemies of the Jews had hoped to overpower them, the opposite occurred, in that the Jews themselves overpowered those who hated them. The Jews gathered together in their cities throughout all the provinces of King Ahasuerus to lay hands on those who sought their harm. And no one could withstand them, because fear of them fell upon all people."* (Esther 9:1-2)

The Jewish men were ready. They were organized and had the king's authority to defend themselves. There was something greater that the people had. The Persians fear of the Hebrew's God. Yes, this unnamed God! God's people need to have a fear of God the Father. *"And thus the secrets of his heart are revealed; and so, falling down on his face, he will worship God and report that God is truly among you."* (I Corinthians 14:25) There is the truth that the fear of God protects those who fear God. This fear was primarily seen from the life of Mordecai.

By the time the original decree was to take effect, those who wished to wipe out the Jews found their positions reversed. Of the hundred million residents in the kingdom, the fifteen million Jewish people now held the upper hand.

This is also illustrated in verses 3-4. *"And all the officials of the provinces, the satraps, the governors, and all those doing the king's work, helped the Jews, because the fear of Mordecai fell upon them. For Mordecai was great in the king's palace, and his fame spread throughout all the provinces; for this man Mordecai became increasingly prominent."* (Esther 9:3-4) The man targeted by Haman for death on the gallows had become a prominent and powerful figure in the nation, and the people actually feared him. This was not his goal or ambition. He was a humble man who only wanted to protect his people, but God rewarded his faithfulness and elevated him to this position.

Notice what happened in verses 5-10. *"Thus the Jews defeated all their enemies with the stroke of the sword, with slaughter and destruction, and did what they pleased with those who hated them. And in Shushan the citadel the Jews killed and destroyed five hundred men. Also Parshandatha, Dalphon, Aspatha, Poratha, Adalia, Aridatha, Parmashta, Arisai, Aridai, and Vajezatha— the ten sons of Haman the son of Hammedatha, the enemy of the Jews—they killed; but they did not lay a hand on the plunder."* (Esther 9:5-10) The Persians that had attacked the Jews had been cooperating with the Amalekite, Haman. The Jewish soldiers were accomplishing what their king Saul had not done years before.

Now the report comes in. The Jews are not the aggressors. Haman's sons are killed! When the feast of Purim takes place and the book of Esther is read all ten names are read with one breath representing that they were killed simultaneously. They killed Haman's sons but were not interested in their goods.

The report to the king, and the remainder of the mission, are recorded in verses 11-16. *"On that day the number of those that were slain in Shushan the palace was brought before the king. And the king said unto Esther the queen, The Jews have slain and destroyed five hundred men in Shushan the palace, and the ten sons of Haman; what have they done in the rest of the king's provinces? now what is thy petition? and it shall be granted thee: or what is thy request further? and it shall be done. Then said Esther, If it please the king, let it be granted to the Jews which are in Shushan to do to morrow also according unto this day's decree, and let Haman's ten sons be hanged upon the gallows. And the king commanded it so to be done: and the decree was given at Shushan; and they hanged Haman's ten sons. For the Jews that were in Shushan gathered themselves together on the fourteenth day also of the month Adar, and slew three hundred men at Shushan; but on the prey they laid not their hand. But the other Jews that were in the king's provinces gathered themselves together, and stood for their lives, and had rest from their enemies, and slew of their foes seventy and five thousand, but they laid not their hands on the prey."* (Esther 9:11-16)

This was a miracle, plain and simple. Our God is a miracle-working God. Remember the mood in Esther 3:15 was quite different. *"The posts went out, being hastened by the king's commandment, and the decree was given in Shushan the palace. And the king and Haman sat down to drink; but the city Shushan was perplexed."* That was when Haman's plan was coming along well, or so he thought.

Contrast that with Esther 8:17. *"And in every province and city, wherever the king's command and decree came, the Jews had joy and gladness, a feast and a holiday. Then many of the people of the land became Jews, because fear of the Jews fell upon them."* What a difference God can make in such a short time.

There is something about the anointing of God on a life, when His hand is upon a man or a woman, which produces fear in other people. I can recall instances at both churches where I served as pastor in which local politicians called to talk about something they were planning to do. I thought, "Why do they care what we think?" It was as if they wanted the blessing of the Christian community on what they were doing. That is the fear of God.

During Jacob's travels we have an example of this in Gen. 35:5. *"And they journeyed, and the terror of God was upon the cities that were all around them, and they did not pursue the sons of Jacob."* The Lord did this again for the children of Israel in Deuteronomy

2:25. *"This day I will begin to put the dread and fear of you upon the nations under the whole heaven, who shall hear the report of you, and shall tremble and be in anguish because of you."* The fear of God protects those who fear Him. I am convinced that, when you go into any given town and find a church that is preaching the gospel, that church is the most important place in that town. People may not agree with it, but they may eventually understand that God is there.

There is something mysterious about the way God works and how He puts His fear upon individuals at certain times. This is true in the case of Haman's sons, whose names were read quickly at the feast following their executions so that no undue recognition was given to them.

An incredible parallel to this story can be found in I Samuel 15 regarding King Saul. Look at verses 10-11. *"Now the word of the Lord came to Samuel, saying, "I greatly regret that I have set up Saul as king, for he has turned back from following Me, and has not performed My commandments. And it grieved Samuel, and he cried out to the Lord all night."*

Samuel prayed all night on Saul's behalf, then went to find him the next day, as we see in verse 12. *"So when Samuel rose early in the morning to meet Saul, it was told Samuel, saying, "Saul went to Carmel, and indeed, he set up a monument for himself; and he has gone on around, passed by, and gone down to Gilgal."* Saul had built a monument to himself. You never read about Mordecai doing anything like that.

The two men came together in verses 13-16. *"Then Samuel went to Saul, and Saul said to him, "Blessed are you of the Lord! I have performed the commandment of the Lord." But Samuel said, "What then is this bleating of the sheep in my ears, and the lowing of the oxen which I hear?" And Saul said, "They have brought them from the Amalekites; for the people spared the best of the sheep and the oxen, to sacrifice to the Lord your God; and the rest we have utterly destroyed." Then Samuel said to Saul, "Be quiet! And I will tell you what the Lord said to me last night." And he said to him, "Speak on."* Samuel was angry here and told Saul to be quiet and hear what he had to say.

Note verses 17-21. *"So Samuel said, "When you were little in your own eyes, were you not head of the tribes of Israel? And did not the Lord anoint you king over Israel? Now the Lord sent you on a mission, and said, 'Go, and utterly destroy the sinners, the Amalekites, and fight against them until they are consumed.' Why then did you not obey the voice of the Lord? Why did you swoop down on the spoil, and do evil in the sight of the Lord?" And Saul said to Samuel, "But I have obeyed the voice of the Lord, and gone on the mission on which the Lord sent me, and brought back Agag king of Amalek; I have utterly destroyed the Amalekites. But the people took of the plunder, sheep and oxen, the best of the things which should have been utterly destroyed, to sacrifice to the Lord your God in Gilgal."*

Saul's attitude was completely wrong. He ultimately lost his kingdom because he was more concerned with the material things he seized from the Amalekites than with obeying and glorifying God. Mordecai and Esther had no interest in the plunder or the spoils.

The second half of Esther 9 describes a great feast created by the Jews to celebrate the success of God's plan. Just as He had a plan in this story, He has one for our time as well.

The Lord has used His chosen people to provide us with His Word. In John 4:4 as Jesus was about to see the Samaritan woman, we read, *"But He needed to go through Samaria."* The gospel was meant for the Samaritans as well as the Jews. As this familiar story shows, the woman at the well became a follower of Christ and went throughout the town telling everyone that she believed she had found the Messiah. Many heard Jesus also and believed because of that.

In Acts 8 it is recorded that Philip preached in Samaria and many came to Christ. It is possible that some of that fruit is due in part to the testimony of the woman at the well. When Cornelius called out to God at the beginning of Acts 10 it was the start of the gospel going to the Gentiles in earnest. The Jews were chosen by God to produce the Word and the Messiah, but now all people from all races have the opportunity to become part of the family of God.

The celebration of the Jews is found in Esther 9:17-32. *"This was on the thirteenth day of the month of Adar. And on the fourteenth day of the month they rested and made it a day of feasting and gladness. But the Jews who were at Shushan assembled together on the thirteenth day, as well as on the fourteenth; and on the fifteenth of the month they rested, and made it a day of feasting and gladness. Therefore the Jews of the villages who dwelt in the unwalled towns celebrated the fourteenth day of the month of Adar with gladness and feasting, as a holiday, and for sending presents to one another. And Mordecai wrote these things and sent letters to all the Jews, near and far, who were in all the provinces of King Ahasuerus, to establish among them that they should celebrate yearly the fourteenth and fifteenth days of the month of Adar, as the days on which the Jews had rest from their enemies, as the month which was turned from sorrow to joy for them, and from mourning to a holiday; that they should make them days of feasting and joy, of sending presents to one another and gifts to the poor. So the Jews accepted the custom which they had begun, as Mordecai had written to them, because Haman, the son of Hammedatha the Agagite, the enemy of all the Jews, had plotted against the Jews to annihilate them, and had cast Pur (that is, the lot), to consume them and destroy them; but when Esther came before the king, he commanded by letter that this wicked plot which Haman had devised against the Jews should return on his own head, and that he and his sons should be hanged on the gallows. So they called these days Purim, after the name Pur. Therefore, because of all the words of this letter, what they had seen concerning this matter, and what had happened to them, the Jews established and imposed it upon themselves and their descendants and all who would join them, that without fail they should celebrate these two days every year, according to the written instructions and according to the prescribed time, that these days should be remembered and kept throughout every generation, every family, every province, and every city, that these days of Purim should not fail to be observed among the Jews, and that the memory of them should not perish among their descendants. Then Queen Esther, the daughter of Abihail, with Mordecai the Jew, wrote with full authority to confirm this second letter about Purim. And Mordecai sent letters to all the Jews, to the one hundred and twenty-seven provinces of the kingdom of Ahasuerus, with words of peace and truth, to confirm these days of Purim at their appointed time, as Mordecai the Jew and Queen Esther had prescribed for them, and as they had decreed for themselves and their descendants concerning matters of their fasting and lamenting. So the decree of Esther confirmed these matters of Purim, and it was written in the book."* A tradition was begun called the feast of Purim, and now they were to gather in Shushan and enjoy all that God was about to do. To this day, when the feast is celebrated and the book of Esther is read, children gather around with special rattles called graggers and they shake them whenever Haman's name is mentioned. This is an important time to remember the deliverance of the Jewish people.

CHAPTER TEN

A HUMBLE CHIEF OPERATING OFFICER

🜲

"*And King Ahasuerus imposed tribute on the land and on the islands of the sea. 2 Now all the acts of his power and his might, and the account of the greatness of Mordecai, to which the king advanced him, are they not written in the book of the chronicles of the kings of Media and Persia? 3 For Mordecai the Jew was second to King Ahasuerus, and was great among the Jews and well received by the multitude of his brethren, seeking the good of his people and speaking peace to all his countrymen.*" (Esther 10:1-3)

These brief three verses remind us that Mordecai used his office to serve the king and to help his fellow Jews. So often a person is placed in authority only to forget their past, their roots, and the people who invested in their lives.

One of the biggest issues for everyone is their money. It is interesting to note that king Ahasuerus institutes a new system of taxation. There are some, including this writer, who believe it is possible that Mordecai had some influence. Peace has arrived in Persia. The people of Israel had a new freedom to work and prosper. Their prosperity would increase the empire's wealth as well as their own holdings. Mordecai reminds the king that the people have a responsibility to their leader.

Here were the Jews in a foreign land, abused, ridiculed, and harassed. Now they were treated fairly. Even though it appears that the Jews would still have threats, Mordecai did his best to be their friend in the government.

Through this episode in the Persian Kingdom God preserves the Jewish people. They should thank Esther and Mordecai. However, the one who orchestrated this entire episode is the Unamed God!

The book of Esther closes with three verses that make up chapter 10. (ASV) *"And the king Ahasuerus laid a tribute upon the land, and upon the isles of the sea. And all the acts of his power and of his might, and the declaration of the greatness of Mordecai, whereunto the king advanced him, are they not written in the book of the chronicles of the kings of Media and Persia? For Mordecai the Jew was next unto king Ahasuerus, and great among the Jews, and accepted of the multitude of his brethren, seeking the wealth of his people, and speaking peace to all his seed."*

Let's look at four lessons this book is teaching us for our lives as well as those who lived through it.

God's Word is eternal – don't box God in. If we are not careful, sometimes we try to become our own scholars and figure out what God is going to do. God works in unusual ways and we must never limit Him. I believe that when we stop trusting in the power, might and omnipotence of God we put limitations on what God wants to do in our lives.

Sometimes you might hear a person give a testimony about a great miracle in his or her life and think to yourself, "Wow, I wish that would happen to me." Don't box God in. Anything can happen.

I have students come into my office all the time with these wonderful plans they have for life and ministry. I never discourage them even though nine out of ten times their plans aren't even doable. But they are dreaming. They are excited. I remember as a college student going to see some of my college professors and telling them my thoughts, and I could tell by looking at them that they weren't buying it, either. But they encouraged me.

You never know what God is about to do in your life. We have a God who works in mysterious and wonderful ways, and when He does so, it isn't always according to the norm. Today we have a generation gap just as we always have had, and part of the reason is that the next generation always sees things a little bit differently from the previous one. If we are not careful, we can squelch what the younger generation is thinking about, when God may just be working a slightly different way in their lives.

The story of Esther is the same way. If you or I had come up with the story of Esther, I don't think any of us would have imagined it like this. Likewise, if we were left to write the story of redemption and salvation, most of us would have incorporated something that in some way involved working your way to Heaven. That would make more sense to our finite minds, but in reality it doesn't make sense when you understand total depravity and how lost we really are. So don't try to make God into what you think He should be. Let Him become in your life what He really is.

God's leading in life is essential. College students ask me all the time, "How do you know that God is leading in your life and it's not someone else leading you?" God's leading is usually prompted by the time we spend in His Word. It doesn't matter how old or young we are; God still wants to lead our lives.

Recently I talked to a 72-year-old man who just received his master's degree. I asked him what he was going to do, and he said he was going to the mission field.

"Who are you going with?" I asked.

"None of the mission agencies will take me," he said. "I'm just going on my own."

Who am I to tell him not to do that? When God is directing us, there is no limit to what can happen. Who would have thought that Esther and Mordecai's story would have ended up the way it did except for the hand of God? When God says something to you in secret and you know it to be true, don't let others talk you out of what God wants you to do.

When I was president of Davis College in New York while also serving as pastor of New Testament Baptist Church in Miami, God spoke to me and told me I should move to Binghamton and spend the rest of my life training young men and women for ministry. I left south Florida in January, when the weather is paradise, and went to upstate New York at a time when the weather is the opposite of paradise. Why would I do that? God was leading me.

Mordecai did not care about being elevated to prime minister, but God led him that way. We must all look at our lives and know that the leading of God is essential.

Always keep your eye on Israel. It fascinates me how many people want to wipe the nation of Israel off the face of the earth. Throughout history, there has constantly been another Haman rising to the forefront. There will be others after him, rising up and doing what they can do to stop Israel in its tracks.

Evangelical Christians and all Americans should understand that there is a promise given by God to Israel, and God will see that promise to its end. If we bless Israel, God will bless us. I want the blessing of God.

Haman had a brilliant plan. The king was on his side, and it seemed as if he could not be stopped. It failed for the simple reason that God made a promise to Israel.

I believe we are living in an age during which if we reach out to Israel, God will honor us for it, especially since we may be close to the return of our Lord.

On one recent trip to Israel I was invited to speak in a synagogue. I began by saying, "I want you to know without any reservation that I am an evangelical Christian. Jesus Christ is the risen Savior and my Lord. I know you don't believe that, but I want you know that we love you without any conditions."

The audience applauded, because they are looking to us for friendship. Our nation needs to be a friend to Israel. Whenever you see or hear something on the news about Israel, pay attention to what is happening there, because God is doing some great things.

God's providence is evident throughout the Bible and in your life. I remind people constantly to watch what God is doing. It is inescapable; if you watch enough, you will see the mighty hand of God. It is always a good idea, as Bible teacher Henry Blackaby has said, to get in the middle of what God is doing.

I was speaking a few years ago at a convention in Orlando, Florida and we were told that a space shuttle launch was scheduled for that day. We all walked outside to watch, because in Orlando you can see the launch about 50 miles away on the Atlantic coast.

As we gathered to watch, a couple of times we heard someone say, "There it is!" Each time it turned to be a commercial jet or a propeller plane. Finally we saw the shuttle, and there was no doubt that it was the real deal. You could see the flame as it soared upward into the sky. It was obvious that something unique had just taken place. We went back inside and talked about what we had just seen.

Sometimes, you might be looking for God and at first you think it is Him, but is only like the jet plane or the prop plane. However, when God is truly at work, you will know it. He is always at work in our nation, in the world, in Israel, and in our churches.

Let me challenge you today always be people of God who are watching God at work. We should not be busy just for the sake of being busy. We should always strive to see the mighty hand of God working in our lives. In Esther, He is not mentioned! But believe me He was there!

A FINAL WORD

This volume on Esther is different. It is not centered on the characters of the book. With all due respect for many excellent volumes this one centers on the unnamed God!

Most studies on Esther center on this queen and her cousin Mordecai. On several occasions in various Bible conferences I delivered a series of sermons on the entire book of Esther. As I prepared and delivered these messages I was overwhelmed with this intriguing story. One day it hit me! This book is about God! He is always at work. His purposes are fulfilled.

When I look back at my own life I am amazed at God's direction. There are many occasions when I was clueless. I had my own agenda and told God how things were supposed to work. Yet as I grow in the latter years of life I am astounded at how God works and accomplishes numerous things that I had no idea of!

God puts stops in our lives. God moves new people in our lives. God lovingly nudges us. He sometimes disciplines us. He is God!

I asked three of my friends to briefly share how God worked in their lives. Dan Rathmell is the President's Assistant at Davis College. He oversees my speaking schedule, travels extensively for our college and has contacts with and knowledge of more pastors in the Northeastern United States than anyone I know. His wife developed frontal lobe dementia at the age of 59. How does anyone go through such an event. Read my colleagues thoughts from his heart.

A remarkable couple is Jack and Joan Heintz of South Florida. I had the honor of being their pastor for nearly 15 years. Jack is a German and Joan is a Russian Jew. Their lives are a story of the amazing God working bringing them together. Jack oversees a wonderful ministry Peace for Israel and he and I have collaborated together on a booklet "Israel Get Ready" with nearly 50,000 in print. I do not know a couple who love Israel more than Jack and Joan.

There are certain testimonies that grip my heart. Go with me to a library! A businessman looking through the business section...What's this? A book out of place on the shelf on the life of the apostles? Read what happened to my dear friend and trustee of Davis College, Michael Houlihan.

In God's unique way...a message from a man's sweetheart with dementia encouraging him, a German/Jew couple in love with Israel's Messiah, Israel's land, and beautifully touching hundreds of lives and a businessman's life changed with a misplaced book in a library. Who orders these things? It is this God who is always at work!

Now how about your life? We are all sinners in need of a Savior. The only Savior from sin is Jesus Christ. The evidence is that He rose from the grave. He is alive and desires to work in your life. Look to what your circumstances are. Whether it is a Jewish queen in a Persian empire married to a man who has no respect for God, a faithful servant whose wife is permanently hospitalized, a couple from two totally different backgrounds or a misplaced book for a businessman, believe me – God is always at work!

HE WAS THERE
DAN RATHMELL

One of my favorite songs is "He was there all the time". For over two years I just didn't see the outward evidence, in my wife, of the truth in the words to this Christian song.

On Sunday, June 13, 2010, two days after our sixth child's wedding, my 59 year old wife woke up crying. This was the first indication that something was wrong. Over the ensuing 443 days, she was in and out of hospitals for five months, and by September 28, 2011, she was admitted to a nursing home. Her diagnosis: Frontotemporal Dementia (FTD). Her doctor said there are over seventy kinds of dementia and this was "the worst kind". Since September 2010, our conversations were seldom better than a parroting of my words; communication with my life partner was essentially gone.

I firmly believe that once a person puts their faith and trust in the Lord Jesus, the Holy Spirit indwells and never leaves that believer (Romans 8:38-39). "He was there all the time" is in reference to the Holy Spirit's permanent presence. I didn't doubt that He lived within her, but I no longer saw outward evidence.

Then, on Mother's Day 2013, an amazing thing happened. I received a note my wife wrote from the nursing home:

Dear Dan,

I, want you to keep the faith

And I want you to keep the faith

and I love you so much I say you so much I want + to keep the faith

This was a "God thing", an outward sign of the ministry of the Holy Spirit I so longed to see. What makes this even more amazing is that my dear wife not only wasn't able to verbalize spiritual things to me, but she also was no longer communicating through writing. My desire has been to finish well, to honor the Lord Jesus through this heartbreaking situation, but I was never able to share this with her. How then was she able to write this note? He was there all the time!

THE APPLE OF GOD'S EYE!
By Jack Heintz

After trusting the Lord Jesus Christ many years ago, I was called by God to leave a successful business and begin a ministry of reaching His chosen people, "Israel."

It has truly been amazing to see how God has blessed, especially since I am of German heritage. Shortly after coming to know the Lord, I claimed a verse given to Jeremiah in chapter 33:3: *"Call unto me, and I will show thee great and mighty things, which thou knowest not."*

Some of the blessings have been seeing many of God's chosen people come to know their Messiah, both in America and Israel. One of the greatest on-going blessings that I share is how He has blessed me by meeting my wife Joan over twenty eight years ago as I was preparing for another tour to Israel.

Because of a blessing in finances, I offered to sponsor a Holy Land tour to any one attending our Beth Shalom Bible studies in South Florida who would meet certain qualifications that included regular attendance, the most personal guests, and the most Bible verses memorized. Joan was that person who qualified for the tour, and as a direct result, she afterwards became my wife. This is truly amazing as God brought me (a German), to marry a Russian Jew!

Little did I know that God is always at work when we do not expect the way He is working. Not only is Joan one of God's chosen people, as He describes the Jewish people "...*the apple of His eye.*" (Zechariah 2:10), <u>she is now the apple of my eye!</u>

The verse in Ephesians 2:14 really has special meaning for both of us: *"For he is our peace, who hath made both one, and hath broken down the middle wall of partition between us;"*

THE BOOK OF ESTHER
A Personal Testimony of God's Providential Working
By Michael Houlihan, M.A.

I was raised in a devout and loving, religious home. My father was a blue collar worker and my mother was a creative home-maker who always made ends meet on our meager income. I was the oldest of four children and we were all educated in private schools.

After graduating from college with honors, I accepted a position as a consultant with an executive search firm and within eighteen months I had purchased the firm. My success in the business world was realized far beyond my expectations. Even in my "wilderness wandering," God was graciously, sovereignly, blessing my life. On several occasions as I interviewed executive candidates, sincere Christians had shared with me their faith in Jesus Christ and what it meant to be "born again." These providential "divine appointments" were not accidental, coincidental events, but part of God's plan. From their testimony I understood that I was a sinner and that the free gift of the salvation of my soul could be accomplished if I simply placed my faith in Jesus Christ alone as my personal Savior. Obviously, this was great news, and contrary to what I believed about Christianity, but I had another problem. I wasn't convinced that Jesus of Nazareth could give me that gift because I wasn't convinced that He had actually risen from the dead. At that point in my life, Jesus was simply a great teacher with a love for mankind, but not God the Son who died and rose from the dead to pay the penalty for my sin.

I remember recognizing that all the individuals who had shared their faith with me were enthusiastically convinced of the reality of their "born again" Christianity. Here they were providentially in my office for an interview, and my purpose was to determine their potential for employment with one of my clients. Instead of trying to convince me of their "wonderful-ness," they were sharing with me the love of God for mankind by the life, death and resurrection of Jesus of Nazareth. They were more interested in their faith and my soul than they were in their personal search for professional employment. I know now that Almighty God had another "purpose" in these circumstances. As a Catholic, my religion only happened on Sunday, and yet here they were on a weekday telling me about their Jesus. They were genuinely concerned for me and the destiny of my soul. I was impressed by their confident faith and zeal for their Biblical Christianity. Their lives were really changed.

From their testimony, it was clear that I was absolutely a "sinner" and at that point in my life, I was thoroughly enjoying my "sin" and all the world had to offer. I owned the big house and the big cars, and my life was everything everyone thinks will bring "happiness." Although I was healthy, educated and prospering, I wasn't "happy" with all of the things the world had promised would bring me happiness. That "emptiness" prompted a search for meaning in my life which led to studying the four Gospels. Actually, one of the men who shared his Christianity challenged me to read the Bible and told me that I should begin with the Gospel of John. This was fortunate because I would have started reading with the book of Genesis. After all, who starts reading a book in the middle?

I had never actually read the Bible, and only accepted what my religion told me was true about Christianity. So out of a sense of intellectual honesty, I decided to at least read the Bible for myself. After reading and studying the life of Jesus in the four Gospels, I was left even more skeptical of Jesus' resurrection from the dead. The Bible relates that despite many miracles to substantiate His credentials as the Messiah, all of His followers denied any association with Him at His public crucifixion. The Bible records that the apostle Peter, whom Jesus had appointed as the leader of the apostles, even denied Jesus three times, and the last time Peter even denied Him with a curse. Obviously, the writers of the four Gospels were not "sugar-coating" what they had witnessed.

If Jesus' very own disciples disowned Him at His crucifixion, why should I think that He was the Messiah, the Son of God who rose from the dead? With that discovery, my search for proof of the resurrection in the Bible had pretty much ended. Then one night in the local public library, while searching for another book,

I came across a book which was misfiled on the library bookshelves. It was a book on the lives of the apostles. I know now that the misplaced book was no coincidence, but that the Lord had sovereignly placed that book there for me. I turned to the life of the apostle Peter and discovered that he had died a martyr's death under the persecutions of the Roman emperor Nero. Confronted with recanting his faith in Jesus Christ to save his life, the apostle Peter refused, and requested that he be crucified upside down. History records that the apostle Peter told his executioners that he was "unworthy to die the way Jesus died" and he wanted to be crucified upside down! Rome obliged.

There among the bookshelves in the library, secular history's indelible record shocked my sensibilities. Why was Peter now giving up his life for Jesus? Why not deny Christ as he did three times at the cross and save his life? What could possibly have happened after the crucifixion of Jesus to change Peter's mind to die for his faith in Christ? Obviously, Peter was not now afraid of death. Something extraordinary had happened AFTER the crucifixion that convinced Peter not to fear death, and that he had eternal life.

History records that Peter and all of the other apostles except John died martyr's deaths, proclaiming that they had seen Jesus risen from the dead and they had watched Him ascend into heaven. Do men give up their lives for a lie? Before the cross, they all denied Christ, but after the cross they gave their lives for Him! Peter and all of the apostle's change of behavior and martyrdom established for me the truth of Jesus' resurrection from the dead. Peter was not afraid to die because he had watched Jesus die on the cross and had seen Him alive resurrected from the dead. Peter sealed the truth of his testimony with his own blood. In the local public library, God graciously saved my soul, and through Peter's upside down crucifixion, revealed the truth of the resurrection of the Lord Jesus Christ. Peter's blood, and that of all of those eyewitnesses of Jesus' crucifixion and resurrection, defies any other explanation for their change of faith and martyrdom. Jesus of Nazareth lives...He is the Son of Man, the Son of God...the Christ!

I remember clearly my experience in the library upon realizing the truth of the resurrection of Jesus of Nazareth. All of those who had told me about their faith in Christ unanimously agreed that my only need was to recognize that I was a lost sinner and place my faith in Jesus Christ as my personal Savior. I realize now that, like Esther, Mordecai, Xerxes and Haman, my circumstances were being ordered by the Lord. As I prayed in the library, acknowledged my sin, and accepted Christ's offer to be my personal Savior, I sensed a great burden lift from my heart. The guilt of my sin was removed. I was forgiven and freed from the penalty of my sin! A warm peace and joy flooded my soul. My life now had eternal significance. The Bible teaches that this experience is a spiritual "regeneration." As a result of placing my faith in Christ, I was permanently indwelt by the Holy Spirit. I was "born again" and became a "new creature" in the eyes of God. The very next Sunday I was in church. I had a new love for God and a hunger to study the Scriptures, living my life pleasing to Him. After I was saved, God continued to abundantly bless my life and business for His glory.

WORKS CITED

(1) The Expositor's Bible Commentary, Gaebelin, 1988, pg. 793

(2) The Expositor's Bible Commentary, Gaebelin, 1988, pg. 107, 108, 111

(3) Wiersbe, The Bible Exposition Commentary 2003, pg. 708, Japanese Proverb

(4) Wiersbe, The Bible Exposition Commentary, 2003, pg. 710, Simpson

(5) Henry, Matthew, The Matthew Henry Commentary, pg. 863

(6) Walter Savage Lander (1775-1867) pg. 718

(7) Herodotus, (Book 111, Section 95)

(8) The Expositor's Bible Commentary, Gaebelin, 1988, pg. 780-781

Books by Dr. Dino Pedrone

MENTORING THE NEXT GENERATION

Why do we lack the leaders with the character and skill needed to our homes, communities, businesses, churches and nation? Our present leaders must invest in future leaders. Do you want to make a lasting impact? Invest your time as a mentor. Mentoring is a stewardship of your life experience which you entrust to the next generation. As a mentor you provide "a brain to pick, a shoulder to cry on and a kick in the pants." Encourage your protégé to be the person whom God created and called. Make a lasting difference in the lives of others.
Mentoring the Next Generation...Making a Lasting Difference...
by Dr. R. Peter Mason with Dr. Pedrone
Article
Xulon Press...143 pages...$16.99

HE MUST BE THE ONE

Religion abounds in the world. Why do Christians seem so set on the idea that there is no other way to God but their way? In the ancient book of Colossians of the New Testament there is a short four chapter presentation that addresses this most controversial question. Each section of the book focuses on a relationship with God and an awareness that religion is not enough.

In He Must Be The One the author Dr. Dino Pedrone presents in very practical terms a presentation of the uniqueness of the person and work of Jesus Christ that helps the reader to stay focused on what is really important in our Christian walk. If Jesus is not the one, then religion must diligently be pursued to find a relationship with God. However, if Jesus is the One, it opens a new world to a relationship not just with God but with people.

He Must Be The One...A verse by verse exposition of the book of Colossians
Article
Xulon Press...85 pages...$13.99

WHAT IN THE WORLD IS GOD DOING?

People in our society are constantly searching for the answers to two questions. They want to know who God is and what He is doing in the world today.

The book of Romans contains a wealth of information about who God is and what He is like. From this we can learn about what He is doing and how His people play an important role in His wonderful plan.

In WHAT IN THE WORLD IS GOD DOING? Dr. Dino Pedrone goes through each chapter and verse of the Apostle Paul's letter to the church at Rome and brings to light many practical applications for our lives and the world we live in now.

WHAT IN THE WORLD IS GOD DOING? Is a book that can assist any believer in finding out what the Lord's plan is for this world and how he or she fits into it. The truths explored in these pages can give you guidance that leads to a more fulfilled Christian life. What in the World is God Doing?...A verse by verse study of the book of Romans
Article
Xulon Press...318 pages...$18.99

TRUE I.D.

Each of us has our own unique identity. Your nationality, your gender, your personal appearance, and even the car you drive can tell the world about you.

Your salvation through Jesus Christ identifies you as well. You are in a select group known as the family of God and that membership carries with it certain responsibilities.

The Apostle Paul wrote about this special identity in the book of Ephesians. In TRUE I.D., Dr. Dino Pedrone guides the reader through a comprehensive study of this epistle that will help you at any stage of your Christian life.

TRUE I.D. will help you see what a privilege it is to be a child of God and how rich your life can be as a result of your relationship with Him.

True I.D....A verse by verse study of the book of Ephesians
Article
Xulon Press...215 pages...$17.99

THE INFLUENCE OF PETER

The life of Peter is a familiar story. Either we have been where he has been in our spiritual walk or someone close to us has recently had a similar experience. Peter was amazed about the Rabbi who selected him. The Rabbi was the Messiah. The elation that the Apostle Peter experienced I found in many of the accounts of his conversations with Jesus.

But then he fell. He fell big time. He denied the One who he claimed was the Messiah. Was his life over? If Jesus was the Messiah, would he have another chance? Perhaps the best answer is found in the two epistles he penned. Our experiences, both good and bad, can be used for the glory of God and they become our influence in other's lives. This book, *The Influence of Peter,* is a reminder of this great lesson. Influence is the capacity to cause an effect in a tangible or intangible way. Peter's influence still continues today.

The Influence of Peter...A synopsis of Peter's Life and verse by verse study of 1 and 2 Peter
Article
Xulon Press...154 pages...$14.99

All of the above books can be purchased for just $50.00 (shipping included) through the Davis College bookstore at www. davisbookstore.com

Davis College is a Christian college committed to making an impact on the world for Jesus Christ. For over 100 years, it has been our mission to train men and women to become servant leaders wherever God calls them. On our beautiful campus in Johnson City, New York, we provide a Christian education learning environment built on a biblical worldview.

At Davis College, you'll experience a close-knit community of college students pursuing God together. Whether you are a traditional undergraduate student, an adult learner wanting to complete a degree, or a current high school student looking to get ahead, Davis College works with you one on one to help you reach your goals. Our online Christian college courses and off campus teaching sites accommodate college students who need a more flexible schedule. Come see why Davis College is a college of ministry like no other.

DAVIS COLLEGE – A GREAT PLACE TO LEARN

CPSIA information can be obtained at www.ICGtesting.com
Printed in the USA
BVOW04s2324230414

351494BV00005B/8/P